MINDFULLY MANIFEST YOUR DESIRES
& CO-CREATE YOUR LIFE WITH THE
UNIVERSE, UNCLUTTERED & ON PURPOSE

30 DAY TAKE ACTION JOURNAL

The Energy
of Gratitude
and More

Open Heart

Lauryn Senko

BALBOA.PRESS
A DIVISION OF HAY HOUSE

Balboa Press books may be ordered through booksellers or by contacting:

Balboa Press
A Division of Hay House
1663 Liberty Drive
Bloomington, IN 47403
www.balboapress.com
844-682-1282

Print information available on the last page.

ISBN: 978-1-9822-4203-9 (sc)
ISBN: 978-1-9822-4201-5 (hc)
ISBN: 978-1-9822-4202-2 (e)

Library of Congress Control Number: 2020913324

Balboa Press rev. date: 10/13/2021

CONNECT WITH ME

Instagram.com/ClutterClearingDiva
Facebook.com/ClutterClearingDiva
Website: ClutterClearingDiva.com

Dedication

This book is dedicated to my wonderful husband,
Rob and my beautiful daughter, Christina.

Rob, thank you for believing in me before
I ever did. Thank you for your unwavering
support and encouragement. I love you.

Christina, my beautiful daughter, I love you. Our
collaboration and chats are always fun and inspiring.
I'm so happy to have you as part of my team.

Special Mention

To D'vorah Lansky – Thank you for all your
guidance, inspiration, and knowledge.
Thank you for shining your light and
helping others to shine theirs.

And

To the beautiful heart-centered souls
who have purchased this journal:
It is my hope that it will inspire you to reach
new heights of joy in all areas of your life.

Continue the Journey

CURRENT PUBLICATIONS

**The Energy of Gratitude and More,
30 Day Take Action Journal**
*Mindfully Manifest Your Desires & Co-Create
Your Life with the Universe, Uncluttered & On Purpose.*

Lined Journals with Quotes
**When You Have More To Say, Just Write!
You Were Meant to Shine
Believe In Yourself**

COMING IN 2021

**The Energy of Gratitude and More,
30 Day Take Action Journal**
Digital & Kindle version

E-Courses & Challenges

**21 Day Gratitude Challenge
The "Vibe" (Vision) Board Challenge
The Energy of Gratitude E-Course
Change Your Mindset, Transform Your Life
E-Course**

Inspirational Card Decks

"The Energy of Gratitude and More" Card Deck
Receive daily, uplifting inspiration by pulling a card a day!

A Note

I truly hope this interactive take action journal makes a difference in your life. I hope it inspires you to embrace life more, love yourself more, and that it helps you to grow into the best version of yourself that you can be. Enjoy the journey!

Lauryn
XO

Be Yourself -
You are your
own
individual
with your
own
unique style

Contents

Power Tools and Play Sheets

Energetic Power Tools and Play Sheets

Life is a Journey

When you embrace it, it can be profoundly life-changing.

This is Gratitude With a Twist!

This take action journal will motivate & inspire you to make **gratitude** your new daily practice.

Gratitude *is the best* Attitude

This is Gratitude with a Twist

I've created this book with you in mind. It's everything that I would want to see in a gratitude journal and that's why I created it. I use it too!

This isn't your typical gratitude journal where you quickly and mindlessly write out what you're grateful for and then put it back on the shelf to continue with your day. Have you done that? That used to be me, until I learned the *art of gratitude* and how it can do so much more than I ever thought possible!

This take action journal focuses on the fundamental steps to integrate gratitude into your life at a deeper level. Gratitude cultivates the true *feelings* of being grateful from the core of your being and is a big piece to co-creating with the *Universe and for your growth!

I learned a long time ago that next to taking action, part of the secret to manifesting your desires is through what you *think, say, do,* and *feel.*

---

*Universe – Some people acknowledge this as God, Goddess, Source, Divine, Spirit, Nature, Creator of All That Is; use the name or label that you feel most comfortable with. Throughout this take action journal I use, "Universe."

Thoughts, words, and feelings all carry a vibration. The frequency (clarity) of this vibration, resonates with the Universe and is known as the **Law of Resonance. The Universe mirrors this vibrational frequency back to you as the ***Law of Attraction.

You are always attracting something into your life. Either more of what you want, a love-based vibration: joy, opportunities, perfect solutions, resources, people, better health, harmonious relationships, abundance, success, or more of what you don't want, a fear-based vibration: lack and struggle.

The level of frequency you're currently vibrating at will be determined by the thoughts you're thinking, the words you're speaking, the feelings you're feeling and the actions you're taking or not taking.

––––––––––––

**Law of Resonance - One of the principle laws of the Universe in which your thoughts, belief systems, feelings and emotions vibrate at a certain frequency. The Law of Resonance activates the Law of Attraction.

***Law of Attraction - To put it simply, *"you are what you think"* – what you think, the words you say, your actions all have an impact on what flows "to you". Like attracts like. If you think negative thoughts, you'll attract negative outcomes. Think positive thoughts and you'll attract positive outcomes.

As you make your way through this journal, you will become aware of how gratitude intertwines with and works successfully with both these laws.

By practicing heartfelt gratitude, your vibration rises, and life flows much easier. Your life becomes more fun! When you are in a high vibration, all this happens naturally, and in fact, the Universe will upgrade your experiences in every way, if-you-let-it.

This is where people often falter. Are you always wishing but never achieving? Your dreams and wishes are what keep you motivated to go after what you want. Yet so many people give up on their dreams. Why is that?

The reason often shows up as a form of resistance that can show up as self-sabotaging behaviour. This happens when your subconscious does everything in its power to keep you safe and in your comfort zone. If you are unaware of this, you can remain stuck, repeating the same self-sabotaging patterns, and living your life on auto-pilot. I write more about this throughout this book.

Enter, CLUTTER! More specifically, *mental* and *emotional* clutter! It's this *mind clutter* that clogs up your life and derails all your hard-earned efforts to act on your dreams. Having an ongoing relationship with gratitude will help to dissolve the mental and emotional clutter and amplify your vibration and manifesting efforts.

When you do the inner work and use the myriad of energetic power tools and strategies provided in this book, it can support you in rewiring your brain for a positive mindset, shift your energy and set you up for success! Refer to the **Power Tools and Play Sheets Section** within this take action journal to learn more.

Gratitude is a foundational tool that works on an energetic level. Combining a gratitude practice with mindset strategies and setting intentions is a powerful combination to rewire your brain's neural pathways to think and do things differently. Think positively versus negatively, forgive and release old hurts and heal, open your heart to a deeper relationship within yourself and others and see the gifts from the lessons in your challenges.

This doesn't come naturally for most people. So, having this take action gratitude journal combined with taking small actionable steps and micro-learning, integrates everything into your life more easily. It retrains the brain to cultivate a beautiful gratitude practice, all the while uncovering and healing the root causes for clutter that can last a lifetime!

Throughout this book, there are lessons and journalling exercises. There are daily gratitude practices and easy strategies to implement; I've labelled them, power tools, and play sheets. You'll practice awareness and mindfulness, and with repetition, you'll notice the subtle, positive shifts in your mindset and your energy, and you'll see that reflected in your life. You'll look for solutions instead of perceiving and focusing on the problems, and you'll realize you have endless choices and opportunities ahead of you.

Rather than living your life *mindlessly* on autopilot, wouldn't you rather *mindfully* manifest your life your way?

WHAT YOU THINK, YOU VIBRATE, WHAT YOU VIBRATE, YOU ATTRACT

Abraham Hicks

What Vibe are you Vibing today?

By having a daily gratitude practice, you will:

✓ Cultivate a positive attitude by letting go of the mental and emotional clutter; *being positive is naturally effortless.*

✓ Open yourself up to deeper insights and connection with your soul; *walk your authentic path and become authentically you.*

✓ Become aware and grateful for the abundance you already have in your life. When you are grateful for what you currently have, you naturally elevate your vibration, attracting positive experiences into your life.

✓ Allow and accept compliments from others easily. You'll say, *"thank you,"* with heartfelt gratitude and a genuine feeling of confidence, self-worth, and deservedness.

✓ Allow and accept the help of others without guilt or the feeling that you need to do it alone when support is offered. If you don't allow help from others, unwittingly, you may be energetically pushing away support from the Universe, unaware of all the good the Universe is flowing your way. Stay open and allowing.

"The Law of Allowing" is another Universal Law. One that can be the most difficult to learn, allowing people and circumstances to be who and what they are without judgement.

Be Open to Something New

This 30-day take action gratitude journal is not just a gratitude journal with lines to write on, as I'm sure you have realized by now.

It's learning to manifest your life, mindfully through conscious creation. You are always creating and attracting something into your life; why not have them be positive experiences?

This is gratitude, AMPLIFIED! One that guides you to:

✓ Reconnect with the core Truth of who you are;

✓ Clarity and awareness of abundant opportunities;

✓ Discover "What lights you up;"

✓ Embrace life with confidence;

✓ Take BOLD action to create the experiences you want;

✓ Shift your mindset into one of feeling abundant for all that you have now.

"CELEBRATE WHAT YOU WANT TO SEE MORE OF,
AND MORE OF WHAT YOU WANT WILL SHOW UP."
Thomas J. Peters

Be Open to Something New

Practicing heartfelt gratitude daily will:

✓ Become automatic and effortless with consistency, attracting *synchronicities* into your life;

✓ Bring awareness and mindfulness to every moment. Living in the present is essential for attracting your desires;

✓ Rewire your neural pathways from scarcity thinking and negativity to one of abundance and positivity. You'll look for possible solutions to obstacles versus seeing blocks and feeling stuck.

✓ Reduce mental and emotional clutter:

- negative thinking, self-critical chatter, monkey mind (busy mind), and being unfocused;

- emotions of guilt, fear, worry, doubt, anxiety, frustration, anger, etc.

✓ Open you up to:

- creativity and inspiration;

- feeling peace and harmony within yourself and in your relationships;

- feeling loved and supported by the Universe;

- a deeper connection with your Higher Self and your soul.

Be Open to Something New

The core feelings of heartfelt gratitude will shift your energy and lift your vibration. In turn this positive signal resonates with the Universe mirroring back to you and attracting the positive things you truly want to attract into your life. I like to call it the vibe you are vibing!

This goes back to the questions you can ask yourself in any given moment, *"what thoughts am I thinking? What feelings am I feeling?"* What vibe am I vibing?" Lower thoughts and feelings result in a lower frequency vibrating out into the Universe, and that is what is mirrored back to you in the form of struggle, lack, worry, etc. Higher vibes, equals higher frequency resonating with the Universe and mirroring back positive experiences to support you. In other words…

"LIKE ATTRACTS LIKE"

This is mindfully co-creating your life with the Universe, one step at a time, knowing that with each action you take creates momentum. That momentum creates the space for the new vibrant energy to flow in and continue supporting you each step of the way until you reach your desired goals and dreams. Of course, those goals and dreams can change along the way as you shift and evolve, and that's perfectly okay!

What Clutter is Clogging up Your Life?

Half the challenge of clearing any type of clutter is becoming aware of what and where it is.

The other half is taking action with small steps toward overcoming it.

It doesn't matter how slowly you go, just don't stop!

What Clutter is Clogging up Your Life?

When you are aware of what lies beneath a cluttered life, you can strip away the layers of belief systems, social conditioning, family patterns, and life's experiences that may be holding you back from living your best life. Doesn't that sound wonderful?

Repetition and consistency is key to growth and transformation. Think of your habitual, negative patterns as "ruts in the road" that keep you stuck in the same tracks and moving through life on an unconscious level, in other words, running on auto-pilot!

By integrating positive daily habits, you can rewire your brain, creating new neural pathways that support you, your gratitude journey, and your dreams! With this, the old neural pathways dissolve (the ruts in the road), and positivity becomes your new normal. The old ruts in the road fall away…

How Deeply Rooted is Your Clutter?

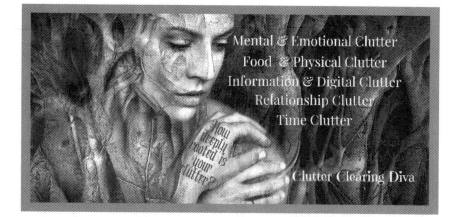

Mental & Emotional Clutter
Food & Physical Clutter
Information & Digital Clutter
Relationship Clutter
Time Clutter

Clutter Clearing Diva

Get into the driver's seat of your own destiny...

Clear your "inner" clutter

Six Types of Clutter

There are six types of clutter to be aware of that can become a problem in your life: Mental and Emotional, Food, Physical, Relationship, Time and Information/digital clutter. However, there is one type especially, that intertwines itself with all other forms of clutter and is the real culprit that can keep you from taking action in your life, and that is mental and emotional clutter.

Mental and emotional clutter and the mindset behind it are one of the most significant pieces to getting unstuck, amplifying your gratitude journey, and manifesting your life on purpose and with more joy. This mindset clutter is the type of clutter that I reference in more detail over the next few pages, and throughout this take action journal. As you move through the 30 days of your journey, you'll understand why.

Food Clutter

Physical Clutter

Relationship Clutter

Time Clutter

Information Clutter

Mental and Emotional Clutter

The following pages provide a brief description of each type of clutter. The short explanation doesn't diminish their importance or the daily issues they can cause in someone's life and being aware of them, can support you through this journey.

Take Action

As you read through the brief descriptions of the different types of clutter that follow, use the journalling pages at the end of this section to write down what insights you receive.

'When you're aware of the underlying reasons for the clutter, you learn to see the gifts - the lessons presented from any situation so you can choose to rise above it and let it go. Once and for all.'

Food Clutter

Harmful eating patterns become engrained habits that, over time may cause a ripple effect of unnecessary weight gain, trouble releasing weight and keeping it off, hormonal imbalances and other health issues over time. The inability to release unwanted weight, is a symptom of underlying health issues; it's not the cause. Focus on becoming healthy, and your body will release the weight.

Four types of eating patterns that can sabotage your weight loss efforts and derail your health:

Emotional Eater: *Self-soother;* your feelings are the trigger which leads to mental and emotional clutter.

Habitual Eater: Busier days, lack of planning, and mindless eating derail your best efforts to eat healthfully.

Addictive Eater: *Sugar and processed carb cravings;* The more you eat them, the more you crave them falling victim to a hi-jacked brain by chemicals such as glucose-fructose, msg (monosodium glutamate) and other substances.

Destructive Eater: *Self sabotager;* you find it difficult to stop overeating, even when you know you're full, sabotaging your hard-earned efforts to lose weight.

Physical Clutter

Physical clutter is often rooted in your emotions (mental and emotional clutter) and may reflect your life experiences that you'd rather keep buried in boxes. When you move houses, you take your STUFF with you instead of dealing with it. Perhaps it's time to face your fears so you can move forward, empowered.

Relationship Clutter

Whether it's friends, family members, or work colleagues, clutter in your relationships can affect your energy in negative ways. It can be emotionally draining, adding mental and emotional clutter to your life. Where are your relationships clogging up your life?

Time Clutter

When your time is cluttered you may find it is filled with meaningless experiences: focusing on the future or the past, may mean you're not mindfully present, leading to mental and emotional clutter; often you put your self-care on the back burner; you're doing, doing, doing and at the end of your day, you feel it's still been non-productive. You may also have a love/hate relationship with time where it is more of a struggle than in the flow.

Information Clutter

Information clutter includes computer, digital, television, and social media. If you obsessively consume a lot of information, you may have what's commonly referred to as FOMO, "fear of missing out." You could also have years of electronic files stored away, without any idea of what they contain. Your social media notifications are all turned on; thousands of emails continue to build up in your inbox from people you may no longer resonate with, and the list goes on!

When you are willing to be open to change, that's when the real journey begins!

Shine Like the Whole Universe is Yours

Rumi

Mental and Emotional Clutter

Mental and emotional clutter is deeply tied to mindset. How you view the world, yourself and others.

Just like *positive* thinking, *negative* thinking can influence your life and the energy that surrounds you, your family, friends, your home, or office in every moment, regardless if you're aware of it or not. Have you become so used to thinking the same thoughts, you don't give any thought to what thoughts you're thinking?

The Subtleties of Mental Clutter;

- Negative thinking;
- Having a negative outlook on life;
- Engaging in critical self-talk, i.e.: putting yourself down; and
- Having "Monkey Mind!" The constant spinning in your head; you're *busy, busy, busy* and find you're easily distracted and unable to focus on one task, ending up with yet another unproductive day.

Sometimes we get so lost, we can't see the forest for the trees. We overlook the simplicity and ease with which we could all be achieving exceptional health and wellbeing.

Mental and Emotional Clutter

The Subtleties of Emotional Clutter;

- Your days are cluttered with the emotions of worry, anxiety, fear, sadness, frustration, doubt or overwhelm, keeping you from thinking more clearly and experiencing more joy in your life;

- Emotions tied to past situations, whether it has been something recent or from long ago;

- Emotions tied to thinking of your future; things that haven't happened yet, creating unnecessary worry, anxiety, and panic, fear, doubt, etc.; and

- You have items displayed or stored away that if you took the time to look at them, emotions would surface within you that you would rather keep buried.

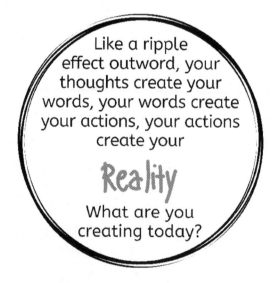

Like a ripple effect outword, your thoughts create your words, your words create your actions, your actions create your

Reality

What are you creating today?

Mental and Emotional Clutter

When you focus on gratitude, there are so many positive shifts that can happen in your life. Your self-love increases, and you learn to approach your situations and challenges from a place of non-judgement, compassion, and love for yourself and others. You'll overcome your challenges without beating yourself up over what you *think* you did wrong, use negative self-talk, or hold onto feelings of guilt, blame, anger, frustration.

Through a daily heartfelt gratitude practice, you can learn how to manage your emotions healthfully, so you can let them go. Everyday make it a practice to be aware of what you **think**, **say**, **feel**, and **do**.

Mental and Emotional Clutter

Mental &
Emotional
Clutter
Weighs
You Down

Thoughts create your words, **words create** your actions, actions create **your reality**.

What thoughts
are you thinking
today?

Clear
your
thought
Clutter

A Journalling Exercise

Reflect: If mental and emotional clutter were acting as barriers to achieving your goals and dreams, what do you think that mental and emotional clutter is? *Write your thoughts here:*

_____

_____

_____

_____

_____

Based on the above, what are some ideas you could implement to remove any mental and emotional barriers? *Write your ideas down:*

_____

_____

_____

_____

_____

_____

AWARENESS IS KEY – BE AWARE & THEN TAKE ACTION

Mental and Emotional Clutter

When you are feeling bogged down emotionally with a situation or challenge, it's not always easy to step away from it and give it some "soak time." However, often this is a necessary step so you can free your mind from the internal struggle that you may be actively engaging in.

When you notice you're placing judgement on yourself, others, or situations of any kind, adopt the saying *"oh that's interesting,"* and then let the thoughts go. Using this phrase keeps your energy *expansive* vs. constrictive, and it's one of many *power* tools I use regularly.

Having an awareness of when you're struggling and noticing the thoughts and emotions as they come up is the first step toward taking action. I've included a six-step action plan to help guide you through any obstacles you may come up against throughout your 30-day journey and beyond.

Refer to the guide, **"Daily Guide to Taking Action,"** located within the Power Tools of the Power Tools and Play Sheets Section. I've also included a graphic of the steps that you can copy and keep with you for easy reference!

Refer to the power tool, "Oh, That's Interesting," in the Power Tools and Play Sheets section to learn more.

When you Have More to Say . . .

Just Write _____

_____

_____

_____

_____

_____

_____

_____

_____

_____

_____

_____

_____

_____

Six Types of Clutter – Journalling Exercise

Food Clutter: As you read the descriptions on food clutter, and the, "Four types of eating patterns that can sabotage your weight loss efforts and derail your health", what insights did you receive about your own eating habits?

_____

_____

_____

_____

_____

_____

_____

_____

_____

_____

_____

_____

In Your Difficulties, Lies Your Opportunities

Be
Obsessively
Grateful

The energy behind the daily gratitude practices is powerful, and works in ways you won't be aware of. Just know it's happening and keep going.

How to Use This
Take Action Journal

This 30 Day Take Action Journal, sets the foundation to help you make positive changes toward living a life filled with more love, joy, ease and flow.

Consider it the daily handbook you won't want to go anywhere without!

what's important is not how fast you go through this book, but how committed you are to your growth and the journey!

How to Use This Take Action Journal

Gratitude Pages: The daily gratitude pages are laid out two days per page except for the fifth day, which includes a beautiful inspirational graphic and quote. Choose a time that works best for you to take a few minutes to write out five things you feel deeply grateful for each day. This practice deepens your connection with your gratitude experience and the energy surrounding it.

The days are numbered in a continuous progression from 1 to 30 for each day of your journey. Keep your momentum going with the daily gratitude practice, even if you need to *"push pause"* temporarily, on the rest of this take action journal.

This take action journal is a 30-day journey, but it's important to remember that this is your journey. Go through it at a pace that feels right for you. It doesn't matter if it takes you 30 days, or longer, as long as you are consistent with *something* to keep your momentum going.

List of Gratitude Prompts: There may be days where feelings of gratitude may be challenging. When your day is less than *vibrant*, refer to the list, "**Gratitude Prompts**," located in the **Power Tools and Play Sheets Section**.

Often, getting started with the prompts is enough to inspire you and you won't need the prompts to finish writing as you feel yourself shift into one of heartfelt gratitude.

"IN THE MIDDLE OF EVERY DIFFICULTY, LIES OPPORTUNITY."
Albert Einstein

Power Tools and Play Sheets Section: The *magic* happens when you are consistent with these practices every day. When you are, they can:

✓ Be fun and easy to integrate into your life.

✓ Shift your energy and rewire your brain for a more positive mindset.

✓ Help you better understand your connection to your past.

✓ Help you uncover where you may have clutter hiding in your life.

✓ Help you to overcome any obstacles and open up your manifestation abilities.

Become familiar with the **Power Tools and Play Sheets Section** of this take action journal. Incorporate them into your life regularly to experience continued growth.

As you become familiar with them, you'll know which ones to use when the need arises. Let your intuition guide you to the perfect power tool and play sheet every time. Work through every section of this book at a pace that feels right for you. One day on a whim, you may want to flip this book open with the intention of integrating into your day whatever is on the page. Intend that every day is a learning opportunity!

The energetic power tools, play sheets and daily expressions of heartfelt gratitude, build upon each other. Include new exercises with current ones, or switch them out for other ones, integrating them all into your life and building momentum.

What seems like effort now will become *effortless* in the days to come, I promise!

Self-Reflection Sections and Journalling Pages:

After every fifth gratitude day (refer to the gratitude journalling pages), there are weekly reflection questions and journalling pages. After completing the Gratitude Section, Days 1 – 30, there is a section called, "30 Days of Reflection Summary." This section will help you summarize your most significant changes, shifts and insights that took place for you since you began this journey. Feel free to use it as you progress through this book.

Capturing your thoughts, feelings, insights, and anything else that surfaces is an essential practice for your awareness and growth. If you don't capture these moments, you'll forget all the positive ways you have shifted, or even worse, you won't notice them at all!

The energy of your gratitude practices and journalling sections is amplified by becoming aware of your thoughts, feelings, and actions. Go through the journalling exercises when you can put a few minutes aside to focus on it. Decide what day works best each week and then put it on your calendar as a reminder to do them.

Uncover the magic that is within you by making it a practice to journal regularly. Check out the three lined journals I've published with inspirational quotes and a special bonus inside of each! All of them are ready to enhance and support you on your life's journey:

When You Have More to Say, Just Write!
You Were Meant to Shine
Believe In Yourself

Make The Most From What You Learn

Whether you are just waking up to your soul journey, or you've been on it for a while, this take action journal will give you tools to learn how to mindfully manifest your life on purpose and with more joy.

Information: The information in this book gives you the knowledge and the tools to take small actionable steps toward making positive changes in your life.

Integration: To make the information meaningful for you, think about how each action step you take relates to you now. How would you like to see your life change? Use the exercises and journaling prompts to do the inner work necessary for growth and transformation to take place.

Practice: The key to any transformation is taking action. By being consistent with the methods you learn in this take action journal, you'll create positive habits that can last a lifetime.

Consistency: When you stay consistent with your practices, you're creating new habits and with new habits you'll see the results happen! Keep taking those small action steps for your transformation and growth.

This 30-day take action journal will bring awareness to everything you do, think, feel and speak so that you can live your life on a conscious level and in gratitude.

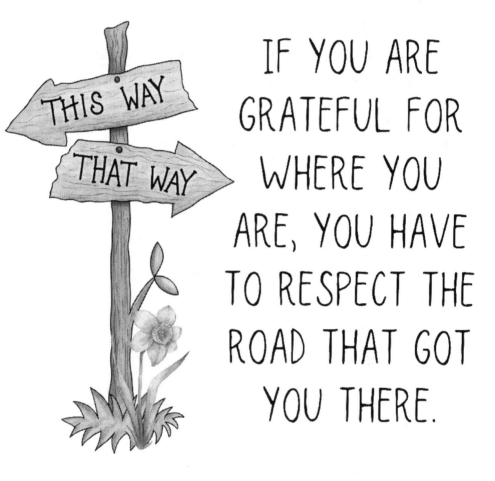

IF YOU ARE GRATEFUL FOR WHERE YOU ARE, YOU HAVE TO RESPECT THE ROAD THAT GOT YOU THERE.

Gratitude Section
Days 1 - 30

We have to keep walking our own path, keep writing our own story, and trust that it will all unfold - not necessarily in our way, but in the way that is for our highest and best good.

Power Tools and Play Sheets

Energetic Power Tools and Play Sheets

Day 1   Date_____

Today I Am Grateful for . . .

1. _____

2. _____

3. _____

4. _____

What can I celebrate myself for today? *Big or small wins, it all counts.*

_____

Day 2   Date_____

Today I Am Grateful for . . .

1. _____

2. _____

3. _____

4. _____

What can I celebrate myself for today? *Big or small wins, it all counts.*

_____

Day 3

Date_____

Today I Am Grateful for . . .

1. _____

2. _____

3. _____

4. _____

What can I celebrate myself for today? *Big or small wins, it all counts.*

_____

Day 4

Date_____

Today I Am Grateful for . . .

1. _____

2. _____

3. _____

4. _____

What can I celebrate myself for today? *Big or small wins, it all counts.*

_____

Day 5

Date_____

Today I Am Grateful for . . .

1. _____

2. _____

3. _____

4. _____

What can I celebrate myself for today? *Big or small wins, it all counts.*

_____

Tip! Incorporate the power tools and play sheets every day and reap the benefits they provide.

The Energy of
GRATITUDE
together with FAITH
is a magical
combination

When you Have More to Say . . .

Just Write _____

_____

_____

_____

_____

_____

_____

_____

_____

_____

_____

_____

_____

Express Gratitude

Weekly Reflections

The exercises are labelled "weekly," appearing every five days, not seven, as the focus is on 30 days. Go at the pace that works for you.

Use the Power Tools and Play Sheets consistently. They are an essential piece to seeing the positive and lasting changes you visualize yourself living.

Weekly Reflections

On the next page is a fun exercise to become aware of all the blessings surrounding you.

When you are open to feeling more gratitude for all that you already have in your life – there is always more that will flow into your life.

Gratitude raises your vibration, utilizing both the Law of Resonance (what you're feeling; the frequency you are vibing) and the Law of Attraction (thoughts, words, actions, including feelings) magnetizing to you, that which you've been focusing on.

More GRATITUDE means less clutter...

...less mental and emotional clutter; (more confidence, focus, clarity, happiness)

...less food clutter (better health and wellbeing);

...less physical clutter (more free flowing energy);

...less relationship clutter (more meaningful relationships);

...less time clutter (more mindfulness, quality presence);

...less information clutter (more creativity, inspiration, better focus.)

GRATITUDE REQUIRES MINDFULNESS AND PRACTICE

Weekly Reflections

Take Action: **Train your brain to look for all things you have to be grateful for, no matter how big or small.** *It could be as simple as something you've become aware of!*

What did you like BEST about this week?

_____

_____

_____

_____

_____

_____

_____

What SILLY thing can you be GRATEFUL for this week?

_____

_____

Why?

_____

_____

Weekly Reflections

What LITTLE thing can you be grateful for this week?

_____

_____

Why?

_____

_____

What CHALLENGING thing can you be grateful for this week?

_____

_____

Why?

_____

_____

What AWARENESS did you have about yourself that you can be grateful for this week?

_____

_____

Why?

_____

_____

Weekly Reflections

If there are any sections or pages that you would like to review again, record them here to refer to.

_____

_____

_____

Prepare for the Week Ahead!

If you're ready, what other energetic power tools or play sheets would you like to include in the upcoming week? Refer to the Power Tools and Play Sheets Section. _Record them here and then create your reminders as described in the power tool, "Gratitude pop ups."_

_____

_____

_____

Pep Talk!

It takes time to build up new positive habits, so go easy on yourself and take it at a pace that works for you. Remember this is your journey!

If you come up against unexpected blocks or what feels like resistance (struggle) vs. feeling light and easy, make sure to do the journalling exercises, power tools and play sheets. You're doing great!

Weekly Reflections

Synchronicities

Synchronicities, also known as coincidences to some, are usually answers to requests made by you to the Universe, directly or indirectly, a conversation you may have had with someone or a thought in your mind.

Have you ever wondered...

How to receive help with something? Who could you receive support from, for something? Where to find the answers to a question? Then, almost like magic, the answers have shown up seemingly out of thin air? Or, perhaps you overheard a conversation that gave you the answers?

Being mindfully present and practicing awareness every day is essential to capturing these synchronicities. Then take action on the option that is the perfect solution for your situation. This is what is known as being in the flow with the Universe!

Take Action

On the following page, capture the synchronicities you've been aware of this week by writing them down.

Journalling about the synchronicities you notice, trains your brain to become more aware of them when they appear.

Weekly Reflections

Synchronicities – Journalling Exercise

What synchronicities appeared this week that have helped you take action? *Write them down:*

_____

_____

_____

_____

_____

How did they help you?

_____

_____

_____

_____

Capturing as many synchronicities as you can each week, even the seemingly insignificant ones will help you when you get to the summary section at the end of this take action journal!

When you Have More to Say . . .

Just Write _____

_____

_____

_____

_____

_____

_____

_____

_____

_____

_____

_____

_____

Life Is Beautiful

Weekly Reflections

Challenges

*Life includes challenges and adversities of all kinds.
In our trials, lies our growth. Within our growth,
lies our epiphanies and transformation.*

It's how we perceive the problem as well as the solution that determines whether we struggle with it or let it flow with little or no resistance.

When we shift our focus from the problem to being open to possible solutions, our brain will seek them out. Now that you're open to solutions showing up ask the Universe for help! Be aware of any synchronicities that appear; they could be the perfect answers you're seeking.

Writing about your challenges can spark possible solutions and open you up to allowing the Universe to flow resources and opportunities your way.

There is always something positive that comes out of any challenging situation. Look for the blessings; focus on that. Be grateful for what you've learned from it, and move forward feeling empowered.

Attract the perfect solutions instead of struggling with the problem. Refer to the Play Sheet, "Seeking Solutions" and the power tool, "I Wonder," in the Power Tools and Play Sheets Section of this book!

Weekly Reflections

Challenges – Journalling Exercise

Describe any challenges you may have had this week. *Writing about them trains your brain to work the situation out and attract the perfect solution.*

_____

_____

_____

_____

_____

If you did know the solution to your situation, what do you think that would be? *Jot down everything that comes to mind; whether you think it's a viable solution or not.*

_____

_____

_____

_____

_____

_____

Reset Your Mindset, Reset Your Life

When you Have More to Say . . .

Just Write _____

_____

_____

_____

_____

_____

_____

_____

_____

_____

_____

_____

_____

_____

What You Appreciate, Appreciates You

Weekly Reflections

Acknowledge, Honour, Celebrate

What specifically can you acknowledge yourself for this week? *Big or small, honour yourself for it and celebrate with a "High Five!" Capture them here!*

_____

_____

_____

_____

_____

_____

_____

When you're co-creating with the Universe to manifest your ideal reality, it's important to acknowledge and celebrate yourself for every step you take forward! Feel heartfelt gratitude and love for yourself and how far you've come. Feel worthy and deserving of success!

Day 6   Date_____

Today I Am Grateful for . . .

1. _____

2. _____

3. _____

4. _____

What can you celebrate yourself for today? *Big or small wins, it all counts.*

_____

Day 7   Date_____

Today I Am Grateful for . . .

1. _____

2. _____

3. _____

4. _____

What can you celebrate yourself for today? *Big or small wins, it all counts.*

_____

Day 8   Date_____

Today I Am Grateful for . . .

1. _____

2. _____

3. _____

4. _____

What can you celebrate yourself for today? *Big or small wins, it all counts.*

_____

Day 9   Date_____

Today I Am Grateful for . . .

1. _____

2. _____

3. _____

4. _____

What can you celebrate yourself for today? *Big or small wins, it all counts.*

_____

Day 10   Date_____

Today I Am Grateful for . . .

1. _____

2. _____

3. _____

4. _____

What can you celebrate yourself for today? *Big or small wins, it all counts.*

_____

Tip! Incorporate the power tools and play sheets every day and reap the benefits they provide.

YOU HAVE THE INNATE ABILITY TO FEEL AND KNOW WHAT ELEVATES YOUR ENERGY AND WHAT BRINGS IT DOWN...

Tune In

When you Have More to Say . . .

Just Write _____

_____

_____

_____

_____

_____

_____

_____

_____

_____

_____

_____

Express Gratitude

Weekly Reflections

"The struggle ends when gratitude begins."

Neale Donald Walsh

Weekly Reflections

On the next page is a fun exercise to become aware of all the blessings surrounding you.

When you are open to feeling more gratitude for all that you already have in your life – there is always more that will flow into your life.

Gratitude raises your vibration, utilizing both the Law of Resonance (what you're feeling; the frequency you are vibing) and the Law of Attraction (thoughts, words, actions, including feelings.)

More GRATITUDE means less clutter...

...less mental and emotional clutter; (more confidence, focus, clarity, happiness)

...less food clutter (better health and wellbeing);

...less physical clutter (more free flowing energy);

...less relationship clutter (more meaningful relationships);

...less time clutter (more mindfulness, quality presence);

...less information clutter (more creativity, inspiration, better focus.)

GRATITUDE REQUIRES MINDFULNESS AND PRACTICE

Weekly Reflections

Take Action: Train your brain to look for all things you have to be grateful for, no matter how big or small. *It could be as simple as something you've become aware of!*

What did you like BEST about this week?

_____

_____

_____

_____

_____

_____

_____

What SILLY thing can you be GRATEFUL for this week?

_____

_____

Why?

_____

_____

Weekly Reflections

What LITTLE thing can you be grateful for this week?

_____

_____

Why?

_____

_____

What CHALLENGING thing can you be grateful for?

_____

_____

Why?

_____

_____

What AWARENESS did you have about yourself that you can be grateful for this week?

_____

_____

Why?

_____

_____

Weekly Reflections

If there are any sections or pages that you would like to review again, record them here to refer to.

_____

_____

_____

Prepare for the Week Ahead!

If you're ready, what other energetic power tools or play sheets would you like to include in the upcoming week? Refer to the Power Tools and Play Sheets Section. _Record them here and then create your reminders as described in the power tool, "Gratitude pop ups."_

_____

_____

_____

Pep Talk!

It takes time to build up new positive habits, so go easy on yourself and take it at a pace that works for you. Remember this is your journey!

If you come up against unexpected blocks or what feels like resistance (struggle) vs. feeling light and easy, make sure to do the journalling exercises, power tools and play sheets. You're doing great!

Weekly Reflections

Synchronicities

Synchronicities, also known as coincidences to some, are usually answers to requests made by you to the Universe, directly or indirectly, a conversation you may have had with someone or a thought in your mind.

Have you ever wondered...

How to receive help with something? Who could you receive support from, for something? Where to find the answers to a question? Then, almost like magic, the answers have shown up seemingly out of thin air? Or, perhaps you overheard a conversation that gave you the answers?

Being mindfully present and practicing awareness every day is essential to capturing these synchronicities. Then take action on the option that is the perfect solution for your situation. This is what is known as being in the flow with the Universe!

Take Action

On the following page, capture the synchronicities you've been aware of this week by writing them down.

Journalling about the synchronicities you notice, trains your brain to become more aware of them when they appear.

Weekly Reflections

Synchronicities – Journalling Exercise

What synchronicities appeared this week that have helped you take action? *Write them down:*

_____

_____

_____

_____

_____

How did they help you?

_____

_____

_____

_____

Capturing as many synchronicities as you can each week, even the seemingly insignificant ones will help you when you get to the summary section at the end of this take action journal!

When you Have More to Say . . .

Just Write _____

_____

_____

_____

_____

_____

_____

_____

_____

_____

_____

_____

Be Authentically, Soulfully You

Weekly Reflections

Challenges

Life includes challenges and adversities of all kinds. In our trials, lies our growth. Within our growth, lies our epiphanies and transformation.

It's how we perceive the problem as well as the solution that determines whether we struggle with it or let it flow with little or no resistance.

When we shift our focus from the problem to being open to possible solutions, our brain will seek them out. Now that you're open to solutions showing up ask the Universe for help! Be aware of any synchronicities that appear; they could be the perfect answers you're seeking.

Writing about your challenges can spark possible solutions and open you up to allowing the Universe to flow resources and opportunities your way.

There is always something positive that comes out of any challenging situation. Look for the blessings; focus on that. Be grateful for what you've learned from it, and move forward feeling empowered.

Attract the perfect solutions instead of struggling with the problem. Refer to the Play Sheet, "Seeking Solutions" and the power tool, "I Wonder," in the Power Tools and Play Sheets Section of this book!

Weekly Reflections

Challenges – Journalling Exercise

Describe any challenges you may have had this week. *Writing about them trains your brain to work the situation out and attract the perfect solution.*

_____

_____

_____

_____

_____

If you did know the solution to your situation, what do you think that would be? *Jot down everything that comes to mind; whether you think it's a viable solution or not.*

_____

_____

_____

_____

_____

Reset Your Mindset, Reset Your Life

When you Have More to Say . . .

Just Write _____

_____

_____

_____

_____

_____

_____

_____

_____

_____

_____

_____

_____

_____

Love Yourself More

Weekly Reflections

Acknowledge, Honour, Celebrate

What specifically can you acknowledge yourself for this week? *Big or small, honour yourself for it and celebrate with a "High Five!" Capture them here!*

_____

_____

_____

_____

_____

_____

_____

When you're co-creating with the Universe to manifest your ideal reality, it's important to acknowledge and celebrate yourself for every step you take forward! Feel heartfelt gratitude and love for yourself and how far you've come. Feel worthy and deserving of success!

Day 11   Date_____

Today I Am Grateful for . . .

1. _____

2. _____

3. _____

4. _____

What can you celebrate yourself for today? *Big or small wins, it all counts.*

_____

Day 12   Date_____

Today I Am Grateful for . . .

1. _____

2. _____

3. _____

4. _____

What can you celebrate yourself for today? *Big or small wins, it all counts.*

_____

Day 13   Date_____

Today I Am Grateful for . . .

1. _____

2. _____

3. _____

4. _____

What can you celebrate yourself for today? *Big or small wins, it all counts.*

_____

Day 14   Date_____

Today I Am Grateful for . . .

1. _____

2. _____

3. _____

4. _____

What can you celebrate yourself for today? *Big or small wins, it all counts.*

_____

Day 15

Date_____

Today I Am Grateful for . . .

1. _____

2. _____

3. _____

4. _____

What can you celebrate yourself for today? *Big or small wins, it all counts.*

_____

Tip! Incorporate the power tools and play sheets every day and reap the benefits they provide.

A
grateful heart
is a
magnet for
miracles

When you Have More to Say . . .

Just Write _____

_____

_____

_____

_____

_____

_____

_____

_____

_____

_____

_____

_____

Express Gratitude

Weekly Reflections

The exercises are labelled "weekly," appearing every five days, not seven, as the focus is on 30 days. Go at the pace that works for you.

Use the Power Tools and Play Sheets consistently. They are an essential piece to seeing the positive and lasting changes you visualize yourself living.

Weekly Reflections

On the next page is a fun exercise to become aware of all the blessings surrounding you.

When you are open to feeling more gratitude for all that you already have in your life – there is always more that will flow into your life.

Gratitude raises your vibration, utilizing both the Law of Resonance (what you're feeling; the frequency you are vibing) and the Law of Attraction (thoughts, words, actions, including feelings.)

More GRATITUDE means less clutter...

...less mental and emotional clutter; (more confidence, focus, clarity, happiness)

...less food clutter (better health and wellbeing);

...less physical clutter (more free flowing energy);

...less relationship clutter (more meaningful relationships);

...less time clutter (more mindfulness, quality presence);

...less information clutter (more creativity, inspiration, better focus.)

GRATITUDE REQUIRES MINDFULNESS AND PRACTICE

Weekly Reflections

Take Action: Train your brain to look for all things you have to be grateful for, no matter how big or small. *It could be as simple as something you've become aware of!*

What did you like BEST about this week?

_____

_____

_____

_____

_____

_____

_____

What SILLY thing can you be GRATEFUL for this week?

_____

_____

Why?

_____

_____

Weekly Reflections

What LITTLE thing can you be grateful for this week?

_____

_____

Why?

_____

_____

What CHALLENGING thing can you be grateful for?

_____

_____

Why?

_____

_____

What AWARENESS did you have about yourself that you can be grateful for this week?

_____

_____

Why?

_____

_____

Weekly Reflections

If there are any sections or pages that you would like to review again, record them here to refer to.

_____

_____

_____

Prepare for the Week Ahead!

If you're ready, what other energetic power tools or play sheets would you like to include in the upcoming week? Refer to the Power Tools and Play Sheets Section. *Record them here and then create your reminders as described in the power tool, "Gratitude pop ups."*

_____

_____

_____

Pep Talk!

It takes time to build up new positive habits, so go easy on yourself and take it at a pace that works for you. Remember this is your journey!

If you come up against unexpected blocks or what feels like resistance (struggle) vs. feeling light and easy, make sure to do the journalling exercises, power tools and play sheets. You're doing great!

Weekly Reflections

Synchronicities

Synchronicities, also known as coincidences to some, are usually answers to requests made by you to the Universe, directly or indirectly, a conversation you may have had with someone or a thought in your mind.

Have you ever wondered...

How to receive help with something? Who could you receive support from, for something? Where to find the answers to a question? Then, almost like magic, the answers have shown up seemingly out of thin air? Or, perhaps you overheard a conversation that gave you the answers?

Being mindfully present and practicing awareness every day is essential to capturing these synchronicities. Then take action on the option that is the perfect solution for your situation. This is what is known as being in the flow with the Universe!

Take Action

On the following page, capture the synchronicities you've been aware of this week by writing them down.

Journalling about the synchronicities you notice, trains your brain to become more aware of them when they appear.

Weekly Reflections

Synchronicities – Journalling Exercise

What synchronicities appeared this week that have helped you take action? *Write them down:*

_____

_____

_____

_____

_____

How did they help you?

_____

_____

_____

_____

Capturing as many synchronicities as you can each week, even the seemingly insignificant ones will help you when you get to the summary section at the end of this take action journal!

When you Have More to Say . . .

Just Write _____

_____

_____

_____

_____

_____

_____

_____

_____

_____

_____

_____

_____

Live Your Most Vibrant Life

Weekly Reflections

Challenges

Life includes challenges and adversities of all kinds. In our trials, lies our growth. Within our growth, lies our epiphanies and transformation.

It's how we perceive the problem as well as the solution that determines whether we struggle with it or let it flow with little or no resistance.

When we shift our focus from the problem to being open to possible solutions, our brain will seek them out. Now that you're open to solutions showing up ask the Universe for help! Be aware of any synchronicities that appear; they could be the perfect answers you're seeking.

Writing about your challenges can spark possible solutions and open you up to allowing the Universe to flow resources and opportunities your way.

There is always something positive that comes out of any challenging situation. Look for the blessings; focus on that. Be grateful for what you've learned from it, and move forward feeling empowered.

Attract the perfect solutions instead of struggling with the problem. Refer to the Play Sheet, "Seeking Solutions" and the power tool, "I Wonder," in the Power Tools and Play Sheets Section of this book!

Weekly Reflections

Challenges – Journalling Exercise

Describe any challenges you may have had this week. *Writing about them trains your brain to work the situation out and attract the perfect solution.*

_____

_____

_____

_____

_____

If you did know the solution to your situation, what do you think that would be? *Jot down everything that comes to mind; whether you think it's a viable solution or not.*

_____

_____

_____

_____

_____

Reset Your Mindset, Reset Your Life

When you Have More to Say . . .

Just Write _____

_____

_____

_____

_____

_____

_____

_____

_____

_____

_____

_____

_____

_____

When I Play, I Let Go Of Worry

Weekly Reflections

Acknowledge, Honour, Celebrate

What specifically can you acknowledge yourself for this week? *Big or small, honour yourself for it and celebrate with a "High Five!" Capture them here!*

_____

_____

_____

_____

_____

_____

_____

When you're co-creating with the Universe to manifest your ideal reality, it's important to acknowledge and celebrate yourself for every step you take forward! Feel heartfelt gratitude and love for yourself and how far you've come. Feel worthy and deserving of success!

Day 16   Date_____

Today I Am Grateful for . . .

1. _____
2. _____
3. _____
4. _____

What can you celebrate yourself for today? *Big or small wins, it all counts.*

_____

Day 17   Date_____

Today I Am Grateful for . . .

1. _____
2. _____
3. _____
4. _____

What can you celebrate yourself for today? *Big or small wins, it all counts.*

_____

Day 18   Date_____

Today I Am Grateful for . . .

1. _____

2. _____

3. _____

4. _____

What can you celebrate yourself for today? *Big or small wins, it all counts.*

_____

Day 19   Date_____

Today I Am Grateful for . . .

1. _____

2. _____

3. _____

4. _____

What can you celebrate yourself for today? *Big or small wins, it all counts.*

_____

Day 20

Date_____

Today I Am Grateful for . . .

1. _____

2. _____

3. _____

4. _____

What can you celebrate yourself for today? *Big or small wins, it all counts.*

_____

Tip! Incorporate the power tools and play sheets every day and reap the benefits they provide.

Always Keep Dreaming!

When you Have More to Say . . .

Just Write _____

_____

_____

_____

_____

_____

_____

_____

_____

_____

_____

_____

_____

_____

_____

Express Gratitude

Weekly Reflections

"Everything has it's beauty,
but not everyone sees it."

Andy Warhol

Weekly Reflections

On the next page is a fun exercise to become aware of all the blessings surrounding you.

When you are open to feeling more gratitude for all that you already have in your life – there is always more that will flow into your life.

Gratitude raises your vibration, utilizing both the Law of Resonance (what you're feeling; the frequency you are vibing) and the Law of Attraction (thoughts, words, actions, including feelings.)

More GRATITUDE means less clutter...

...less mental and emotional clutter; (more confidence, focus, clarity, happiness)

...less food clutter (better health and wellbeing);

...less physical clutter (more free flowing energy);

...less relationship clutter (more meaningful relationships);

...less time clutter (more mindfulness, quality presence);

...less information clutter (more creativity, inspiration, better focus.)

WHAT YOU APPRECIATE, APPRECIATES YOU

Weekly Reflections

Take Action: **Train your brain to look for all things you have to be grateful for, no matter how big or small.** *It could be as simple as something you've become aware of!*

What did you like BEST about this week?

_____

_____

_____

_____

_____

_____

_____

What SILLY thing can you be GRATEFUL for this week?

_____

_____

Why?

_____

_____

Weekly Reflections

What LITTLE thing can you be grateful for this week?

_____

_____

Why?

_____

_____

What CHALLENGING thing can you be grateful for?

_____

_____

Why?

_____

_____

What AWARENESS did you have about yourself that you can be grateful for this week?

_____

_____

Why?

_____

_____

Weekly Reflections

If there are any sections or pages that you would like to review again, record them here to refer to.

_____

_____

_____

Prepare for the Week Ahead!

If you're ready, what other energetic power tools or play sheets would you like to include in the upcoming week? Refer to the Power Tools and Play Sheets Section. _Record them here and then create your reminders as described in the power tool, "Gratitude pop ups."_

_____

_____

_____

Pep Talk!

It takes time to build up new positive habits, so go easy on yourself and take it at a pace that works for you. Remember this is your journey!

If you come up against unexpected blocks or what feels like resistance (struggle) vs. feeling light and easy, make sure to do the journalling exercises, power tools and play sheets. You're doing great!

Weekly Reflections

Synchronicities

Synchronicities, also known as coincidences to some, are usually answers to requests made by you to the Universe, directly or indirectly, a conversation you may have had with someone or a thought in your mind.

Have you ever wondered...

How to receive help with something? Who could you receive support from, for something? Where to find the answers to a question? Then, almost like magic, the answers have shown up seemingly out of thin air? Or, perhaps you overheard a conversation that gave you the answers?

Being mindfully present and practicing awareness every day is essential to capturing these synchronicities. Then take action on the option that is the perfect solution for your situation. This is what is known as being in the flow with the Universe!

Take Action

On the following page, capture the synchronicities you've been aware of this week by writing them down.

Journalling about the synchronicities you notice, trains your brain to become more aware of them when they appear.

Weekly Reflections

Synchronicities – Journalling Exercise

What synchronicities appeared this week that have helped you take action? *Write them down:*

_____

_____

_____

_____

_____

How did they help you?

_____

_____

_____

_____

Capturing as many synchronicities as you can each week, even the seemingly insignificant ones will help you when you get to the summary section at the end of this take action journal!

When you Have More to Say . . .

Just Write _____

_____

_____

_____

_____

_____

_____

_____

_____

_____

_____

_____

_____

_____

Life Is Beautiful

Weekly Reflections

Challenges

Life includes challenges and adversities of all kinds. In our trials, lies our growth. Within our growth, lies our epiphanies and transformation.

It's how we perceive the problem as well as the solution that determines whether we struggle with it or let it flow with little or no resistance.

When we shift our focus from the problem to being open to possible solutions, our brain will seek them out. Now that you're open to solutions showing up ask the Universe for help! Be aware of any synchronicities that appear; they could be the perfect answers you're seeking.

Writing about your challenges can spark possible solutions and open you up to allowing the Universe to flow resources and opportunities your way.

There is always something positive that comes out of any challenging situation. Look for the blessings; focus on that. Be grateful for what you've learned from it, and move forward feeling empowered.

Attract the perfect solutions instead of struggling with the problem. Refer to the Play Sheet, "Seeking Solutions" and the power tool, "I Wonder," in the Power Tools and Play Sheets Section of this book!

Weekly Reflections

Challenges – Journalling Exercise

Describe any challenges you may have had this week. *Writing about them trains your brain to work the situation out and attract the perfect solution.*

_____

_____

_____

_____

_____

If you did know the solution to your situation, what do you think that would be? *Jot down everything that comes to mind; whether you think it's a viable solution or not.*

_____

_____

_____

_____

_____

_____

Stay Centered In Gratitude

When you Have More to Say . . .

Just Write _____

_____

_____

_____

_____

_____

_____

_____

_____

_____

_____

_____

_____

Live Your Most Vibrant Life

Weekly Reflections

Acknowledge, Honour, Celebrate

What specifically can you acknowledge yourself for this week? *Big or small, honour yourself for it and celebrate with a "High Five!" Capture them here!*

_____

_____

_____

_____

_____

_____

_____

When you're co-creating with the Universe to manifest your ideal reality, it's important to acknowledge and celebrate yourself for every step you take forward! Feel heartfelt gratitude and love for yourself and how far you've come. Feel worthy and deserving of success!

Day 21   Date_____

Today I Am Grateful for . . .

1. _____
2. _____
3. _____
4. _____

What can you celebrate yourself for today? *Big or small wins, it all counts.*

_____

Day 22   Date_____

Today I Am Grateful for . . .

1. _____
2. _____
3. _____
4. _____

What can you celebrate yourself for today? *Big or small wins, it all counts.*

_____

Day 23   Date_____

Today I Am Grateful for . . .

1. _____

2. _____

3. _____

4. _____

What can you celebrate yourself for today? *Big or small wins, it all counts.*

_____

Day 24   Date_____

Today I Am Grateful for . . .

1. _____

2. _____

3. _____

4. _____

What can you celebrate yourself for today? *Big or small wins, it all counts.*

_____

Day 25

Date_____

Today I Am Grateful for . . .

1. _____

2. _____

3. _____

4. _____

What can you celebrate yourself for today? *Big or small wins, it all counts.*

_____

Tip! Incorporate the power tools and play sheets every day and reap the benefits they provide.

THE ROOT OF
ALL GRATEFULNESS
IS GRATITUDE

When you Have More to Say . . .

Just Write _____

_____

_____

_____

_____

_____

_____

_____

_____

_____

_____

_____

Express Gratitude

Weekly Reflections

The exercises are labelled "weekly," appearing every five days, not seven, as the focus is on 30 days. Go at the pace that works for you.

Use the Power Tools and Play Sheets consistently. They are an essential piece to seeing the positive and lasting changes you visualize yourself living.

Weekly Reflections

On the next page is a fun exercise to become aware of all the blessings surrounding you.

When you are open to feeling more gratitude for all that you already have in your life – there is always more that will flow into your life.

Gratitude raises your vibration, utilizing both the Law of Resonance (what you're feeling; the frequency you are vibing) and the Law of Attraction (thoughts, words, actions, including feelings.)

More GRATITUDE means less clutter...

...less mental and emotional clutter; (more confidence, focus, clarity, happiness)

...less food clutter (better health and wellbeing);

...less physical clutter (more free flowing energy);

...less relationship clutter (more meaningful relationships);

...less time clutter (more mindfulness, quality presence);

...less information clutter (more creativity, inspiration, better focus.)

WHAT VIBE ARE YOU VIBING?

Weekly Reflections

Take Action: Train your brain to look for all things you have to be grateful for, no matter how big or small. *It could be as simple as something you've become aware of!*

What did you like BEST about this week?

_____

_____

_____

_____

_____

_____

_____

_____

What SILLY thing can you be GRATEFUL for this week?

_____

_____

Why?

_____

_____

Weekly Reflections

What LITTLE thing can you be grateful for this week?

_____

_____

Why?

_____

_____

What CHALLENGING thing can you be grateful for?

_____

_____

Why?

_____

_____

What AWARENESS did you have about yourself that you can be grateful for this week?

_____

_____

Why?

_____

_____

Weekly Reflections

If there are any sections or pages that you would like to review again, record them here to refer to.

_____

_____

_____

Prepare for the Week Ahead!

If you're ready, what other energetic power tools or play sheets would you like to include in the upcoming week? Refer to the Power Tools and Play Sheets Section. _Record them here and then create your reminders as described in the power tool, "Gratitude pop ups."_

_____

_____

_____

Pep Talk!

It takes time to build up new positive habits, so go easy on yourself and take it at a pace that works for you. Remember this is your journey!

If you come up against unexpected blocks or what feels like resistance (struggle) vs. feeling light and easy, make sure to do the journalling exercises, power tools and play sheets. You're doing great!

Weekly Reflections

Synchronicities

Synchronicities, also known as coincidences to some, are usually answers to requests made by you to the Universe, directly or indirectly, a conversation you may have had with someone or a thought in your mind.

Have you ever wondered...

How to receive help with something? Who could you receive support from, for something? Where to find the answers to a question? Then, almost like magic, the answers have shown up seemingly out of thin air? Or, perhaps you overheard a conversation that gave you the answers?

Being mindfully present and practicing awareness every day is essential to capturing these synchronicities. Then take action on the option that is the perfect solution for your situation. This is what is known as being in the flow with the Universe!

Take Action

On the following page, capture the synchronicities you've been aware of this week by writing them down.

Journalling about the synchronicities you notice, trains your brain to become more aware of them when they appear.

Weekly Reflections

Synchronicities – Journalling Exercise

What synchronicities appeared this week that have helped you take action? *Write them down:*

_____

_____

_____

_____

_____

How did they help you?

_____

_____

_____

_____

Capturing as many synchronicities as you can each week, even the seemingly insignificant ones will help you when you get to the summary section at the end of this take action journal!

When you Have More to Say . . .

Just Write _____

_____

_____

_____

_____

_____

_____

_____

_____

_____

_____

_____

_____

_____

Gratitude Is The Fuel Of The Universe

Weekly Reflections

Challenges

Life includes challenges and adversities of all kinds. In our trials, lies our growth. Within our growth, lies our epiphanies and transformation.

It's how we perceive the problem as well as the solution that determines whether we struggle with it or let it flow with little or no resistance.

When we shift our focus from the problem to being open to possible solutions, our brain will seek them out. Now that you're open to solutions showing up ask the Universe for help! Be aware of any synchronicities that appear; they could be the perfect answers you're seeking.

Writing about your challenges can spark possible solutions and open you up to allowing the Universe to flow resources and opportunities your way.

There is always something positive that comes out of any challenging situation. Look for the blessings; focus on that. Be grateful for what you've learned from it, and move forward feeling empowered.

Attract the perfect solutions instead of struggling with the problem. Refer to the Play Sheet, "Seeking Solutions" and the power tool, "I Wonder," in the Power Tools and Play Sheets Section of this book!

Weekly Reflections

Challenges – Journalling Exercise

Describe any challenges you may have had this week. *Writing about them trains your brain to work the situation out and attract the perfect solution.*

_____

_____

_____

_____

_____

If you did know the solution to your situation, what do you think that would be? *Jot down everything that comes to mind; whether you think it's a viable solution or not.*

_____

_____

_____

_____

_____

_____

Reset Your Mindset, Reset Your Life

When you Have More to Say . . .

Just Write

Only Look Back To See How Far You've Come

Weekly Reflections

Acknowledge, Honour, Celebrate

What specifically can you acknowledge yourself for this week? *Big or small, honour yourself for it and celebrate with a "High Five!" Capture them here!*

_____

_____

_____

_____

_____

_____

_____

When you're co-creating with the Universe to manifest your ideal reality, it's important to acknowledge and celebrate yourself for every step you take forward! Feel heartfelt gratitude and love for yourself and how far you've come. Feel worthy and deserving of success!

Day 26   Date_____

Today I Am Grateful for . . .

1. _____

2. _____

3. _____

4. _____

What can you celebrate yourself for today? *Big or small wins, it all counts.*

_____

Day 27   Date_____

Today I Am Grateful for . . .

1. _____

2. _____

3. _____

4. _____

What can you celebrate yourself for today? *Big or small wins, it all counts.*

_____

Day 28   Date_____

Today I Am Grateful for . . .

1. _____

2. _____

3. _____

4. _____

What can you celebrate yourself for today? *Big or small wins, it all counts.*

Day 29   Date_____

Today I Am Grateful for . . .

1. _____

2. _____

3. _____

4. _____

What can you celebrate yourself for today? *Big or small wins, it all counts.*

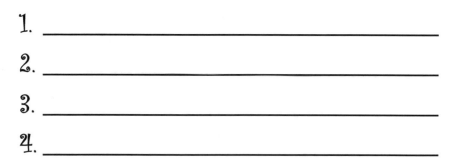

Day 30   Date_____

Today I Am Grateful for . . .

1. _____

2. _____

3. _____

4. _____

What can you celebrate yourself for today? *Big or small wins, it all counts.*

_____

Tip! Incorporate the power tools and play sheets every day and reap the benefits they provide.

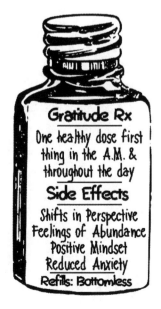

When you Have More to Say . . .

Just Write _____

_____

_____

_____

_____

_____

_____

_____

_____

_____

_____

_____

_____

_____

Express Gratitude

Weekly Reflections

Stay present in the moment, Open to receiving, Anchored in gratitude.

Weekly Reflections

On the next page is a fun exercise to become aware of all the blessings surrounding you.

When you are open to feeling more gratitude for all that you already have in your life – there is always more that will flow into your life.

Gratitude raises your vibration, utilizing both the Law of Resonance (what you're feeling; the frequency you are vibing) and the Law of Attraction (thoughts, words, actions, including feelings.)

More GRATITUDE means less clutter...

...less mental and emotional clutter; (more confidence, focus, clarity, happiness)

...less food clutter (better health and wellbeing);

...less physical clutter (more free flowing energy);

...less relationship clutter (more meaningful relationships);

...less time clutter (more mindfulness, quality presence);

...less information clutter (more creativity, inspiration, better focus.)

BE MINDFULLY PRESENT AND CENTERED IN GRATITUDE

Weekly Reflections

Take Action: **Train your brain to look for all things you have to be grateful for, no matter how big or small.** *It could be as simple as something you've become aware of!*

What did you like BEST about this week?

_____

_____

_____

_____

_____

_____

_____

What SILLY thing can you be GRATEFUL for this week?

_____

_____

Why?

_____

_____

Weekly Reflections

What LITTLE thing can you be grateful for this week?

_____

_____

Why?

_____

_____

What CHALLENGING thing can you be grateful for?

_____

_____

Why?

_____

_____

What AWARENESS did you have about yourself that you can be grateful for this week?

_____

_____

Why?

_____

_____

Weekly Reflections

If there are any sections or pages that you would like to review again, record them here to refer to.

_____

_____

_____

Prepare for the Week Ahead!

If you're ready, what other energetic power tools or play sheets would you like to include in the upcoming week? Refer to the Power Tools and Play Sheets Section. _Record them here and then create your reminders as described in the power tool, "Gratitude pop ups."_

_____

_____

_____

Pep Talk!

It takes time to build up new positive habits, so go easy on yourself and take it at a pace that works for you. Remember this is your journey!

If you come up against unexpected blocks or what feels like resistance (struggle) vs. feeling light and easy, make sure to do the journalling exercises, power tools and play sheets. You're doing great!

Weekly Reflections

Synchronicities

Synchronicities, also known as coincidences to some, are usually answers to requests made by you to the Universe, directly or indirectly, a conversation you may have had with someone or a thought in your mind.

Have you ever wondered...

How to receive help with something? Who could you receive support from, for something? Where to find the answers to a question? Then, almost like magic, the answers have shown up seemingly out of thin air? Or, perhaps you've overheard a conversation that gave you the answers?

Being mindfully present and practicing awareness every day is essential to capturing these synchronicities. Then take action on the option that is the perfect solution for your situation. This is what is known as being in the flow with the Universe!

Take Action: On the following page, capture the synchronicities you've been aware of this week by writing them down.

Journalling about the synchronicities you notice, trains your brain to become more aware of them when they appear.

Weekly Reflections

Synchronicities – Journalling Exercise

What synchronicities appeared this week that have helped you take action? *Write them down:*

_____

_____

_____

_____

_____

How did they help you?

_____

_____

_____

_____

Capturing as many synchronicities as you can each week, even the seemingly insignificant ones will help you when you get to the summary section at the end of this take action journal!

When you Have More to Say . . .

Just Write _____

_____

_____

_____

_____

_____

_____

_____

_____

_____

_____

_____

_____

_____

So Much Flows To You Through Gratitude

Weekly Reflections

Challenges

Life includes challenges and adversities of all kinds. In our trials, lies our growth. Within our growth, lies our epiphanies and transformation.

It's how we perceive the problem as well as the solution that determines whether we struggle with it or let it flow with little or no resistance.

When we shift our focus from the problem to being open to possible solutions, our brain will seek them out. Now that you're open to solutions showing up ask the Universe for help! Be aware of any synchronicities that appear; they could be the perfect answers you're seeking.

Writing about your challenges can spark possible solutions and open you up to allowing the Universe to flow resources and opportunities your way.

There is always something positive that comes out of any challenging situation. Look for the blessings; focus on that. Be grateful for what you've learned from it, and move forward feeling empowered.

> Attract the perfect solutions instead of struggling with the problem. Refer to the Play Sheet, "Seeking Solutions" and the power tool, "I Wonder," in the Power Tools and Play Sheets Section of this book!

Weekly Reflections

Challenges – Journalling Exercise

Describe any challenges you may have had this week. *Writing about them trains your brain to work the situation out and attract the perfect solution.*

_____

_____

_____

_____

_____

If you did know the solution to your situation, what do you think that would be? *Jot down everything that comes to mind; whether you think it's a viable solution or not.*

_____

_____

_____

_____

_____

_____

Reset Your Mindset, Reset Your Life

When you Have More to Say . . .

Just Write _____

_____

_____

_____

_____

_____

_____

_____

_____

_____

_____

_____

_____

If You're Not In Control Of Your Thoughts, Who Is?

Weekly Reflections

Acknowledge, Honour, Celebrate

What specifically can you acknowledge yourself for this week? *Big or small, honour yourself for it and celebrate with a "High Five!" Capture them here!*

_____

_____

_____

_____

_____

_____

_____

When you're co-creating with the Universe to manifest your ideal reality, it's important to acknowledge and celebrate yourself for every step you take forward! Feel heartfelt gratitude and love for yourself and how far you've come. Feel worthy and deserving of success!

When you have more to say...

Just Write!

When you let go of the mental and emotional clutter, shift your mindset and practice gratitude, your vibration elevates and you flow effortlessly with the universe!

When you Have More to Say . . .

Just Write _____

_____

_____

_____

_____

_____

_____

_____

_____

_____

_____

_____

_____

_____

_____

Elevate Your Vibe, To Elevate Your Experiences

When you Have More to Say . . .

Just Write _____

_____

_____

_____

_____

_____

_____

_____

_____

_____

_____

_____

_____

Replace Judgement With Compassion

When you Have More to Say . . .

Just Write _____

_____

_____

_____

_____

_____

_____

_____

_____

_____

_____

_____

_____

_____

The Power Is Already Within You

WHEN YOU TAKE ACTION,
IT UNWINDS YOU,
ALLOWING FOR CLARITY
TO UNFOLD.

When you Have More to Say . . .

Just Write _____

_____

_____

_____

_____

_____

_____

_____

_____

_____

_____

_____

_____

Gratitude Is The Best Attitude

When you Have More to Say . . .

Just Write _____

_____

_____

_____

_____

_____

_____

_____

_____

_____

_____

_____

_____

_____

Awareness Is Key, Be Aware & Then Take Action

When you Have More to Say . . .

Just Write _____

_____

_____

_____

_____

_____

_____

_____

_____

_____

_____

_____

_____

_____

What We Think Gets More Powerful

When you Have More to Say . . .

Just Write _____

_____

_____

_____

_____

_____

_____

_____

_____

_____

_____

_____

_____

Live Life Vibrantly

KEEP GOING –
ALLOW FOR THE UNIVERSE
TO CATCH UP WITH YOU
AND JUST KNOW IT WILL.

Shift Your Energy with
with
Power & Play
Tools Sheets

You become
so used to thinking
the same thoughts,
you don't give any
thought to what
thoughts you are
thinking.

Awareness is KEY

Power Tools and Play Sheets

Energetic Power Tools and Play Sheets

Gratitude Prompts

"Gratitude is the fuel of the Universe.
Fill your tank with it and you will go far."
– Radleigh Valentine

Gratitude Prompts

When you have a day that is less than *vibrant*, use these prompts and start writing; soon, you'll feel your energy shift into one of love and gratitude!

- ○ I am grateful for the beauty that surrounds me
- ○ I am grateful for the lakes
- ○ I am grateful for my pet(s): dog/cat/bird etc.
- ○ I am grateful for the love of my family
- ○ I am grateful for the love of my children/spouse
- ○ I am grateful for my home
- ○ I am grateful for my car
- ○ I am grateful for my job/career/business
- ○ I am grateful for help with: _____
- ○ I am grateful for sunshine
- ○ I am grateful for the rain
- ○ I am grateful for seeing a beautiful rainbow
- ○ I am grateful for the trees, grass, flowers
- ○ I am grateful for the abundance in my life
- ○ I am grateful for the loving relationships in my life
- ○ I am grateful for the support of my body
- ○ I am grateful for everything I learned today
- ○ I am grateful for my health
- ○ I am grateful for my friends
- ○ I am grateful for: _____

Daily Guide to Taking Action

TAKING ACTION
GETS YOU MOTIVATED

HABIT
KEEPS YOU GOING

Daily Guide to Taking Action

Six Steps to Moving Forward When You're Feeling Stuck

What lies beneath all types of clutter is most often mental and emotional clutter and the layers of belief systems formed by social conditioning, family patterns, and life's experiences.

They are your *"ruts in the road"* that keep you spinning your wheels and stuck when all you want is to keep moving in the direction of your goals and dreams.

Once you are aware of the different forms of clutter as it appears for you, know that you have the POWER to change it through the choices you make.

Take Action: Throughout this 30-day journey (and beyond), use the guide on the following page to help you take action when you come across a challenging situation or when you become aware that your thoughts and actions aren't in alignment with the daily, positive vibe you're looking to be, feel and have.

Each situation you encounter often triggers different emotions, depending on the root cause. When choosing which energetic power tool or play sheet to use each time, be open to allowing your inner wisdom to guide you to the perfect one!

Daily Guide to Taking Action

1. **AWARENESS**
   - ✓ Be aware of when you are struggling.

2. **IDENTIFY**
   - ✓ Identify the type of clutter that is causing the perceived challenge. Ask yourself, *"what's at the root of this situation?"* Keep asking questions and journal for more insights!

3. **CHOOSE**
   - ✓ Choose (and use) the power tools and play sheets to help you overcome the problem.

4. **HEAL & LET GO**
   - ✓ If something needs healing (a block, limiting beliefs, or a mindset shift); do the necessary inner, self-love *"work"* using the power tools and play sheets available to you in this take action journal.

5. **EXPRESS GRATITUDE** - *This is a <u>key</u> practice.*
   - ✓ What are the *gifts* you've received from this situation? What awareness? Show heartfelt gratitude for where you've been, how far you've come, everything you uncover. Be grateful for it all.

6. **TAKE ACTION**
   - ✓ Now that you've done all that inner work move forward feeling, EMPOWERED!

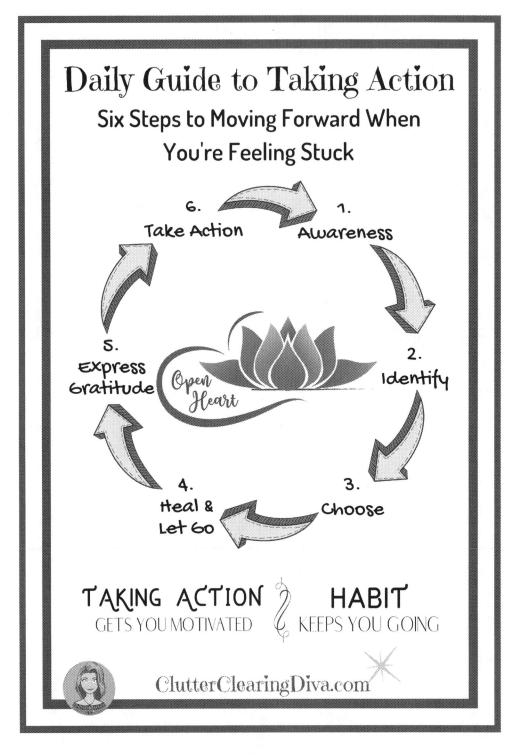

Daily Guide to Taking Action
Six Steps to Moving Forward When You're Feeling Stuck

6. Take Action

1. Awareness

2. Identify

3. Choose

4. Heal & Let Go

5. Express Gratitude

Open Heart

TAKING ACTION
GETS YOU MOTIVATED

HABIT
KEEPS YOU GOING

ClutterClearingDiva.com

Energetic

Power Tools

To Shift Your Energy

Shift

Happens!

Power Tool - Gratitude Pop-ups

Commit to having an "Attitude of Gratitude!"

Practice this exercise until it's effortless!

Gratitude Exercise: Shift your mindset to focus on the positive experiences and things you already have in your life.

When you focus your attention on the positive, your mind is less likely to focus on any feelings of lack or scarcity that would lower your vibration (vibe). As a result, your thoughts, words, and actions naturally become more positive, re-wiring your neural pathways and forming new positive habits. Your positive momentum accelerates, and your vibration continues to rise and match the speed at which your desires vibrate. Life begins to flow with more ease and Grace!

Take Action: Create recurring pop-ups in your calendar and on your cell phone with a gratitude reminder every hour. If every hour seems a little daunting to you, then start with a minimum of three times a day. Try adding one reminder first thing upon waking, again in the afternoon and another before going to bed.

Adjust the number of reminders accordingly, so you don't create any overwhelm. Just make sure to do them with consistency.

If you don't have a computer or cell phone, consider leaving sticky notes with your reminders where you can see them such as on doors, windows, mirrors, and even in your wallet or purse.

When the reminders pop up, or you see one of your notes, take a *heartfelt* moment to *feel* grateful and say, "thank you," in your mind or out loud. It can be for something or someone currently in your life, something you did that day or week. It can be anything. No matter how small the blessings are – it makes a difference to acknowledge them all!

Refer to the "Gratitude Prompts" list in the Power Tools and Play Sheets section of this book if you need help with a prompt or two.

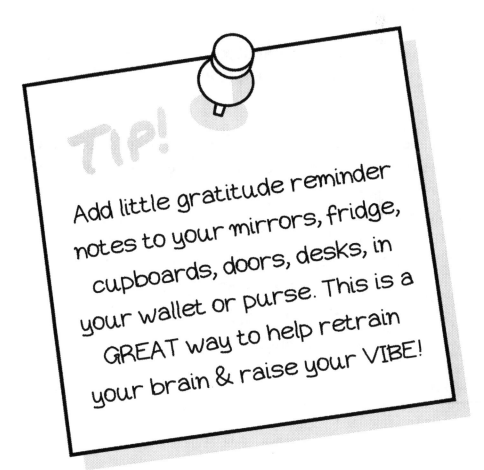

Tip!

Add little gratitude reminder notes to your mirrors, fridge, cupboards, doors, desks, in your wallet or purse. This is a GREAT way to help retrain your brain & raise your VIBE!

Power Tool – Relationship Affirmations

Affirmations are powerful! Repeating affirmations to yourself throughout the day elevates your vibration and frequency and focuses your intention on what you would like to improve upon in your life.

After all, if you're always thinking anyway, they may as well be "happy" thoughts and attract more of the same!

Take Action

Review the brief description, "Relationship Clutter," located in the section, "What Clutter is Clogging up Your Life?"

On the following page, cultivate the habit of regularly repeating the affirmations using the words in the graphic. By doing this, you can bring positive energy into all your relationships.

Example:

All my relationships are loving
All my relationships are uplifting
All my relationships are cherished

All My Relationships are . . .

Loving Uplifting
Cherished Respectful
Genuine Empowering Happy
Replenished Nurturing Joyful
Valued Supportive Energizing
Appreciated Affectionate
Healthy Fun

Power Tool – Oh, That's Interesting

When you become aware that you are judging yourself, others, situations, or you analyze your journalling, refer to this energetic power tool often and stay in the energy of the observer.

Take Action

When you're aware of when you are placing judgement on something, someone, or a situation, say the statement **"oh, that's interesting"** (out loud or in your mind) and then let those thoughts go. Your energy will remain in a neutral state, so you stay in flow with the Universe!

As you make this practice a daily habit, it may surprise you to notice how often you judge, yourself, situations and others around you.

Engaging in the mental and emotional clutter of self-critical thinking and placing judgement on situations, yourself, or others constricts your energy. It's vital to stay in a flowing and expanded state, so use this power tool often!

When you consistently make this a practice, releasing self-critical talk and judgemental thinking, will be a breeze!

Power Tool – I Wonder...

Have you wondered about something, and then almost like magic, the answer appeared? This truly is one of my most fun power tools to use, and it works like magic!

The Practice

Do you need answers? Are you wondering the *how, what, where,* or *why's* of something?

Attract the answers by choosing the phrase below that works best for your situation. Complete the sentence out loud or in your mind:

"I wonder how _____"?

"I wonder where I can find_____"?

"I wonder who I can _____"?

"I wonder what _____"?

Use these phrases or any variation of the above phrases on its own or in tandem with the power tool, ***Seeking Solutions.*** Watch for synchronicities that may hold the answers you're seeking!

Practice Patience

Being aware and open to receiving the answer will keep your energy expansive. Don't obsess over when or how the solution will show up as this creates constrictive, closed off energy. The first few times you try it, think of this exercise as an experiment; *keep it fun, light and easy!*

By posing the question with intention, you are energetically handing your situation over to the care of the Universe. So, let go and let the Universe do its thing! The more you use this tool, the better it works!

Reminder!

WE ARE NOT ON THIS PATH TO FIX

OURSELVES, BUT TO BECOME THE BEST

VERSION OF OURSELVES THAT WE CAN BE.

THERE IS A DIFFERENCE.

Power Tool – Seeking Solutions

Focus On The Solution - Not The Problem

When you are focused on the problem, your brain is FOCUSED ON THE PROBLEM, constricting your energy and making it difficult to attract the perfect solution.

Attract solutions by using the phrases below. You'll stay expansive as your brain looks for that ideal solution. All you need to do is stay aware and open to the perfect answer showing up. The phrases work like setting an intention!

Choose from these examples or create your own:

"**I know** there is a solution for this_____;"

"**I AM open** to receiving the perfect solution showing up;"

"**I wonder** what the solution is for _____?"

"**What would it take** for the perfection solution to show up easily?"

Whether your problems are big or small, use these phrases on their own or with the power tool, "I Wonder." Being consistent and using both power tools, "*Seeking Solutions*," and "*I Wonder*," can maximize the benefits of rewiring your brain and creating new neural pathways. No more "ruts in the road!"

The more you use these tools with INTENTION, the more energetic power is working behind those intentions, and the better it works!

Reminder!

WHEN THE RIGHT SOLUTION SHOWS UP,

REMEMBER TO EXPRESS HEARFELT

GRATITUDE!

Power Tool - You Have the Power!

When you give yourself permission to feel your emotions…

✓ **You have the power** to acknowledge your feelings, work through the healing process and then *let it go;*

✓ **You have the power** to bring your awareness back into the present moment if you're thinking about something in the future or the past;

✓ **You have the power to choose** a different thought that empowers you vs. a disempowering thought;

✓ **You have the power to choose** to perceive any situation through the lens of love;

✓ **You have the power to choose** to remain neutral about a situation, be the observer and come from a place of non-judgement so you can look at it through the lens of love; and

✓ **You have the power to choose** a love-based thought over a fear-based one.

If you are feeling any mental and emotional clutter, acknowledge and release it, never hold it inward. Use the power tools and play sheets to help you move through it.

THE CHANGE YOU'RE LOOKING FOR STARTS FROM WITHIN

When you Have More to Say . . .

Just Write _____

_____

_____

_____

_____

_____

_____

_____

_____

_____

_____

_____

_____

Express Gratitude

Power Tool - 1, 2, 3, Breathe

This breathing exercise is a great "go to" power tool to use any time.

Whenever you feel the mental and emotional clutter of anxiety, stress, worry, panic, or an overly busy mind (any fear-based emotions), your *fight or flight* activates, and your body's self-preservation kicks in. Clear thinking becomes difficult.

This breathing exercise brings your focus back into the present moment, keeping you centered and grounded, calming your nervous system, and clarifying your thinking. You'll remain open to seeing possibilities and solutions.

Calming Breath Exercise: (Read all five steps before trying it)

1. Stand or sit with your shoulders back, chest forward and eyes closed.

2. Smile (or imagine smiling).

3. Breathe in deeply and slowly through your nose to the count of three; 1 – 2 – 3. *Imagine breathing in white light throughout your body.*

4. Hold for a count of three; 1 – 2 – 3.

5. Breathe out slowly through your mouth to the count of three; 1 – 2 – 3. As you do, imagine any fear or any uneasiness leaving your body through the bottoms of your feet and dissolving into Gaia, mother earth.

Repeat this exercise a minimum of three times or until you feel calm and relaxed.

Power Tool - Just Play!

Did you know that "PLAYING" is a POWER TOOL?

When you take time to play, you're taking time for self-care, relationship building and allowing the Universe to jump in and help you attract those things you're trying so hard to bring into your reality.

When you take time to play, you are letting go and allowing the Universe to do its thing without fighting for control.

When you take time to play, you let go of the mental and emotional clutter...the worrying, the doubting, the fears and instead allow yourself to have fun and fully enjoy spending time to play.

Take Action

Take the time to allow PLAY into your life frequently. Feel heartfelt gratitude for yourself, for those you love and for those you are spending time with.

Become aware of the cool synchronicities that show up! All because you took time out to PLAY, you are in RECEIVING mode!

Just Play

when I play, I attract miracles

Power Tool - Just Play!

What does play look like for you?

Write down a few ideas and choose a different one each week to play!

_____

_____

_____

_____

_____

_____

_____

_____

_____

_____

_____

_____

When I Play, I Let Go Of Worry

Power Tool – I AM Power Statements

**"I AM. Two of the most powerful words; for what
you put after them, shapes your reality."
– Dee Wallace**

How often do you use the words **I AM** to define yourself and
your reality? Probably more often than you think, and most
likely in a disempowering way than an empowering way.

Example: Think of phrases such as "I AM not capable" or "I
AM sick and tired." These are two examples of using I AM in a
disempowering way. Remember, what you *think, say, do,* you
attract as your reality. Refer to the section, "This is Gratitude
with a Twist!" for a refresher.

The late, Dr. Wayne Dyer wrote a blog article on the meaning
and energy behind the words I AM. You can find it here: https://
www.drwaynedyer.com/blog/the-power-of-i-am/

Be Aware: When you're thinking negatively or using self-critical
talk, rephrase what you are saying or thinking without using the
words, "I AM" in a disempowering way, as explained above.

When you repeat, **I AM** power statements, you will cultivate
a positive habit of rewiring your brain, create new neural
pathways, and align yourself with your TRUE POWER. Positive
thinking becomes your new baseline!

By using these **I AM** statements on the next page, you stay
aligned with your POWER, for you are the power! You have the

power to choose your thoughts, words, and actions to create your reality.

Feel into the words, and if the phrases feel uncomfortable as you're saying them, then you may have a little work to do on yourself. Repeat them daily until you embody these words and feel the shift in your energy. You can also think up your own **I AM** statements and write them down on the journalling page included.

Suggestion: Use Ho'oponopono, the ancient Hawaiian practice of forgiveness, with yourself as the focus until you feel yourself shift and know that you are loved, and worthy of receiving all the joy and abundance that the Universe is continuously flowing to your way. The Ho'oponopono play sheet is within the play sheets section of this take action journal.

Take Action

On the following page are easy to remember **I AM** statements. The energy behind them is powerful, so repeat them when you feel the downward spiral of mental and emotional clutter or recite them anytime for a POWER BOOST!

"I AM" Power Statements

I AM
POWER

I AM
PEACE

I AM
JOY

I AM
BOLD

I AM WORTHY

I AM
LOVE

I AM
FEARLESS

I AM
INFINITE

I AM
DESERVING

ClutterClearingDiva.com

"I AM" Power Statements
Write Your Own!

I AM Grateful
I AM Enough
I AM Confident
I AM Prosperity

_____

_____

_____

_____

_____

_____

_____

_____

_____

_____

I AM Vibrant Health

"BE WILLING TO TAKE THE FIRST STEP, NO MATTER HOW SMALL IT IS, CONCENTRATE ON THE FACT THAT YOU ARE WILLING TO LEARN. ABSOLUTE MIRACLES WILL HAPPEN."

Louise L. Hay

Shift Your Energy
with
Play Sheets

Play Sheets

My Gratitude Journal

When you let go of the mental and emotional clutter, shift your mindset and practice gratitude, your vibration elevates to flow effortlessly with the Universe.

What you think
you become

*What you feel
you attract*

*What you imagine
you create*

Buddha

Play Sheet

**Think Big
Dream Bigger**

*No one achieves their
dreams by standing still.*

Think Big & Dream Bigger

Instructions

If you knew you could not fail at your dreams, what would they be?

Do you have outrageous dreams and goals?

Great! Write them all down! Resist the temptation to want to figure out the "how." Practice letting go and write them all out anyway.

This is a feel-good practice; so go for it and FEEL GOOD!

Take Action

Use the play sheets, "*Think Big & Dream Bigger*," on the following two pages, write out a list of <u>all</u> your dreams and goals, no matter how outrageous you think they are!

✓ As you write, feel gratitude deep within your heart as if your dreams have already manifested. Visualize the "happy outcome!"

✓ Read them often.

✓ Know and believe that they are possible by taking one step at a time. With each step taken, the next will show up.

✓ Give yourself permission to change them from time to time. As you grow and evolve so will your dreams.

Think Big & Dream Bigger

Journalling Exercise

Part of co-creating with the Universe is to DREAM BIG and imagine achieving those dreams, the "happy outcome." The Universe will bring you the steps you need as you need them.

If you knew you could not fail at your dreams, what would they be? Write them all down on this list and imagine how they will make you feel once you achieve them. *Big and small – list them all!*

_____

_____

_____

_____

_____

_____

_____

_____

_____

Dream Bigger

Think Big & Dream Bigger

Journalling Exercise

Continue with the "Dream Big" journalling exercise. Imagine how it will feel once you achieve them!

Get really detailed about your dreams and desires. *Remember to tweak them as you grow and evolve. Big and small – list them all!*

_____

_____

_____

_____

_____

_____

_____

_____

_____

Dream It, Then Do It

Think Big – Dream Bigger

Dream Bigger_____

_____

_____

_____

_____

_____

_____

_____

_____

_____

_____

_____

_____

_____

What You Imagine, You Create

Think Big – Dream Bigger

Dream Bigger_____

_____

_____

_____

_____

_____

_____

_____

_____

_____

_____

_____

_____

_____

Live Life, Inspired

"What if
I fall?
Oh, but my
darling,
what if
you fly?"

Erin Hanson

Play Sheet

What's a "RAK?"

Random Acts of Kindness

"RAK" is an acronym for *Random Acts of Kindness*. Something you do out of the goodness of your heart for others without expecting anything in return.

Expand your vibration and feel such gratitude for doing something good for others, whether they know of your act of kindness or not. **RAK** also includes "Paying it forward." Have you ever bought a cup of coffee for the stranger in line behind you? Or let someone go ahead of you in the lineup at the grocery store when you see they have a handful of items and you have a full cart?

These are random acts of kindness, and they will bring a genuine smile of gratitude to others for your generosity! Random acts of kindness spread more love energy out into the world, and the Universe always responds in kind.

Take Action

Over the next couple of pages are journalling exercises to help you with becoming a better receiver of RAK and a list of suggested *random acts of kindness* that you can do for others.

RAK LIST

Hold a door open for someone.

Give someone a smile.

Let someone step in front of you in a line-up.

Buy someone a coffee.

Pay someone a compliment.

Run an errand for someone housebound.

Spend time visiting a senior's home:
play games, chat, have coffee.

Visit an animal shelter: *spend time with the animals, donate food, help clean the kennels.*

Do something nice for a friend, your spouse or kids.

Do a random act of kindness for yourself!

In addition to this list, what are other random acts of kindness you can do regularly? *Jot your ideas here!*

_____

_____

_____

_____

What's a "RAK?"

Random Acts of Kindness - Journalling Exercise

"Random Acts of Kindness"

Have you been on the receiving end of random acts of kindness?

Allowing and receiving kindness and support even in the smallest ways from others, expands your energy for the Universal flow of continued support. When you're in the flow of receiving, it happens even before you know you need it!

Take Action

When you become aware of receiving kindness and support, no matter how small the act is, take a moment to feel grateful for it and record those acts on the following journalling pages.

Recognizing each time you receive a kind gesture or support is an awareness exercise that trains your brain to become aware of all the ways you receive kindness and support. It's an opportunity for your subconscious to believe you truly are supported (eliminating self-sabotage and limiting beliefs), and that the Universe really does have your back!

"No act of kindness no matter
how small is ever wasted."
Aesop

What's a "RAK?"

Random Acts of Kindness - Journalling Exercise

Record below any random acts of kindness and support you receive. *Feel heartfelt gratitude for the support you receive!*

_____

_____

_____

_____

_____

_____

_____

_____

_____

_____

_____

RAK Spreads More Love Energy Out Into The World And The Universe Always Responds In Kind!

What's a "RAK?"

Random Acts of Kindness - Journalling Exercise

Continue to record below any random acts of kindness and support you receive.

*Everyone reaps the benefits of **RAK**. It can be as simple as extending out a smile or holding the elevator door for someone.*

_____

_____

_____

_____

_____

_____

_____

_____

_____

There Is Always An Opportunity For Kindness

The Mirror Effect

Your Internal World Reflects Your Outer World

The Mirror Effect

Your Outer World Reflects Your Inner World.

Have you ever noticed that when you run errands, go shopping, walk the dog, or you are around other people, that those people reflect your *"vibe?"*

What you project outward is what you attract. A smile will get you a smile, and a frown will get you a frown. Hence, what's known as the *Mirror Effect.*

When you are smiling, you will see people that are happy and joyful, but if you're frowning and feeling any mental and emotional clutter, you may attract and see people who also aren't in a great mood. It's the Law of Attraction and the Law of Resonance at work.

The opposite can also happen when you give a smile or say hello to someone that's feeling down. You can lift a person's spirits just because they are in the presence of your *good vibrations!*

Having a lower vibe, may have other ripple effects. Think about a time where you left the house, and you were already feeling frustrated.

Have you had the experience of coming upon every possible red light on your way to a meeting, accidentally spilling your coffee while juggling other things in your hands, or missing appointments, all in one afternoon? These are the laws at work – but you have the POWER to change that BEFORE you leave the house.

Take Action

Use the following page to write down a list of ideas to shift your vibration into a place of love, gratitude, and joy before leaving home.

The next time you need a quick pick me up, *you'll have a few ideas to refer to* quickly before *going out.*

To get you started I've listed a few ideas:

- ✓ Listen to a quick 10-minute meditation;
- ✓ Use the power tool, "1, 2, 3, Breathe," located within the *Power Tools section;*
- ✓ Go for a walk around the block reciting "I AM Power Statements, located in the *Power Tools section;*
- ✓ Read a couple of chapters from a motivational book;
- ✓ Watch an inspirational video on YouTube;
- ✓ Listen to beautiful, uplifting music;
- ✓ Journal what's on your mind and then release it;
- ✓ Read inspirational quotes.

IT ALL STARTS WITH ONE SMALL STEP, KEEP GOING!

The Mirror Effect

Journalling Exercise

List your ideas of things you can do to change your mood and uplift your vibe before going out.

_____

_____

_____

_____

_____

_____

_____

_____

_____

_____

_____

_____

What Vibe Are You Vibing?

Play Sheet

Using Symbols As Anchors

Using Symbols as Anchors

The Practice

Using symbols as anchor points and associating them with repeating an affirmation or mantra is a way to rewire your brain to think positively and drop the negative chatter. It shifts your mindset to focus on your intention.

This practice will help your energy stay expansive, so you don't get caught up in a downward spiral of mental and emotional clutter constricting your energy.

Choose Your Symbol

Option 1: Decide on what you would like to use as your symbol – something that you already have and love, (often you associate this symbol with a beautiful memory). Display it where you can look at it often throughout the day, such as on your desk at work or somewhere in a room in your home where you will see it often.

Option 2: Any jewelry works well because you can wear it, touch it and reach for it easily whenever you need it throughout the day.

Option 3: Choose a symbol to set an intention to begin your day on a high vibe and positive note! Put the symbol (anchor) where you will see it upon waking in the morning. Set the intention to have a great day ahead!

Using Symbols as Anchors

The Practice

When you look at your symbol throughout your day (hold it, feel it or think of it if it's not with you), repeat your affirmation (also known as a mantra) as much as possible in your mind or out loud. A couple of times here and there though-out the day adds up! There is no limit to how often you repeat your phrase, just be consistent.

You'll know when this new habit has taken "root" and is anchored, (in other words, you've *retrained your brain*,) when the association you have with your symbol and the affirmation, automatically pop into your head as soon as you look at it.

Water as a Symbol and Anchor Point?

Yes! Every time you pour yourself a glass of water, say an affirmation. Keep the affirmation the same each time you pour yourself a glass of water. When you pour yourself a cup of coffee or tea, use a different affirmation. When you stay consistent, it becomes ingrained in your subconscious activating the universal laws of Attraction and Resonance.

Choose one affirmation or mantra to use with each symbol (anchor) otherwise, you may confuse your brain and the energy behind the intention, and it won't work the way it is intended.

Use symbols as anchor points to ground yourself, reset your energy, and shift your mindset when you need it most.

Use symbols as anchor points to set daily intentions, focus your mind, and set yourself up for a positive day ahead.

Play Sheet

Thoughts, Words, Actions, Oh My!

What Reality Are You Creating Today?

Thoughts, Words, Actions, Oh My!

What Reality Are You Creating Today?

Your thoughts create your words, your words create your actions, your actions create your reality.

The Daily Practice

This daily practice may take a little effort; however, as the saying goes, *"change your thoughts, change your life."* It can and it will make a difference in your reality as you move forward. From all the information you glean from this book, let this be one of the GOLDEN NUGGETS you learn and practice throughout your whole life.

Awareness

If you're not aware of what you are thinking and speaking, then you'll miss all the opportunities to rephrase your thoughts and words as you go through your day.

Awareness is key to what thoughts you are thinking, the words you are speaking, and the actions you are taking.

Rephrase, Rephrase, Rephrase

When you notice you are speaking negatively, being self-critical, or judgemental, whether it's toward yourself, someone else, or even situations, make sure to rephrase!

Thoughts, Words, Actions, Oh My!

What Reality Are You Creating Today?

Easy Ways to Remember this Practice

✓ Create reminders that pop up throughout the day to practice being aware of your thoughts, words, and actions. Adopt the practice of the gratitude pop-ups exercise by setting the reminders as *"what thoughts am I thinking?" What words am I speaking?"* Refer to the play sheet, "Gratitude Pop-ups," in the Power Tools and Play Sheets section.

✓ In addition to the pop-up reminders on your computer and cell phone, place sticky notes where you will see them often; for example, your bathroom mirror, bedroom nightstand, and doors.

✓ Remember to rephrase your negative thoughts, words, and actions into positive ones as often as you are aware of it. This is extremely helpful for rewiring your neural pathways and think more positively.

✓ After rephrasing your thoughts and words, note the differences in how your body and mind feel when you check in with yourself.

IF YOU'RE NOT IN CONTROL OF YOUR
THOUGHTS, THEN WHO IS?

Thoughts, Words, Actions, Oh My!

What Reality Are You Creating Today?

Over time this exercise reduces mental and emotional clutter, dissolves old patterns of negative self-talk, and reinforces beautiful positive habits; habits worthwhile!

Having the awareness to change your thoughts when the mental and emotional clutter sneaks in, is like turning on a light switch in your mind. With consistent practice, this habit becomes effortless!

Being a positive person internally attracts positive people and other positive experiences and opportunities into your life. When positive energy surrounds you, your self-esteem increases, you exude confidence, and you are inspired to take action towards fulfilling your goals and dreams!

> Be consistent and aware.
> Make this a regular practice.

YOUR THOUGHTS CREATE YOUR WORDS,
YOUR WORDS CREATE YOUR ACTIONS,
YOUR ACTIONS CREATE YOUR REALITY.

What will you create today?

Play Sheet

Old Habits & Patterns

The Ruts That Keep You Stuck

Old Habits & Patterns

The Ruts In The Road That Keep You Stuck

Your belief systems are integrated throughout your life and can be identified as the habitual patterns related to your money, health, business, education, relationships, and life in general.

Throughout your childhood, adolescence and adult years, conditioning from family, friends, colleagues, and society (think marketing by large corporations through the internet, radio, television, etc.) all contribute to your belief systems today. A lot of your life experiences are based on belief systems and thought of as true, but are they?

Your habitual patterns, whether you are aware of them or not, begin early in childhood being absorbed into your subconscious, usually before the age of seven. They start with your parents, grandparents, or caregivers. As an example, think about the conversations you may have overheard as a child where your parents mentioned money.

Perhaps you remember hearing them say (or you were told), "Money is hard to come by." "Life is always a struggle." "It's better to give than receive." *Tell me this, how do you give if you are never receiving?*

Think of the airplane scenario: The flight attendants instruct you to put your mask on first in case of an emergency so then you can help others. In other words, fill yourself up first, and then you have plenty to give to others!

If you're not receiving because of an old belief system, through your actions, you may be inadvertently telling the Universe, "no help required, thank you very much!" As you can see, there are many different forms of receiving; it's not only with money.

All this contributes to feeling stuck and living your life on "auto-pilot," stuck in the ruts on the road with your health and well-being, money, relationships, career, and life in general.

Take Action

If you're so inclined, re-read the sections listed below. You'll receive greater clarity and further insights reading it a second or even a third time:

- ✓ Introduction
- ✓ This is Gratitude with a Twist
- ✓ What is Clogging up your life?

Go through the Interactive Meditation and then on the following journalling pages, write down what insights you receive as a result.

Journalling increases your awareness of the habitual patterns (programming) you're repeating through life so you can "Take Action."

INTERACTIVE MEDITATION EXPERIENCE

Instructions

Before preceding to the next page, please read this page first. *Take yourself through this meditation as many times as you like.*

While you do this exercise, play soft calming music to make it easier to relax and focus on this meditation experience.

Step One: Read through the interactive meditation on the next page at least once before taking yourself through it.

Step Two: After reading through the interactive meditation, think about the questions. As you take yourself through the meditation and remember specific events, use the pages that follow to write them down. Then go right back into your meditation.

This isn't a typical meditation, but one where you are interacting with yourself along the way.

It may be helpful to have someone you trust, take you through the meditation experience by having them read out loud the prompts and questions. Have them use a soft, quiet voice to enhance the meditation experience. As they take you through the meditation, have them write down the answers you provide.

INTERACTIVE MEDITATION EXPERIENCE

Take a few minutes to sit comfortably in a quiet place, and close your eyes.

Take three deep breaths, inhaling and exhaling slowly.

Now imagine or picture...

A movie screen appearing before you in your mind...

On the movie screen, you see yourself as a child about the age of five, six, or seven...

How old are you?

Now imagine or picture...

The clothes you're wearing...

What are you wearing?

What colours are the clothes you're wearing?

What is the style of your hair...Is it long or short?

What type of shoes are you wearing, or are you barefooted?

Are you in your house? Or, outside in the yard...Where are you?

Paint as clear a picture for yourself as you can.

INTERACTIVE MEDITATION EXPERIENCE

(Continuing with the Meditation Experience)

What has come up for you? Write down what you've discovered so far and then continue.

With your eyes closed again, imagine your parents, grandparents or caregivers there with you...

What are you doing?

What are they doing?

Are you overhearing a conversation they are having?

What are they saying to each other?

What are they saying to you?

Spend as long as you need with your eyes closed. Imagine this scene as vividly as you can on the movie screen in your mind. Take your time as you remember the details...

When you're ready, bring awareness back to your body, wiggling your toes and fingers...

Take three, slow, deep breaths and open your eyes.

Welcome back!

INTERACTIVE MEDITATION EXPERIENCE

Journalling Exercise

When you're ready, use the space below to journal about your experience. *It may only be pieces of conversations or fragmented stories; that's okay. As you write, more information may come. Make sure to write it down.*

There is more journalling space on the next page.

_____

_____

_____

_____

_____

_____

_____

_____

_____

_____

Replace Judgement With Compassion

When you Have More to Say . . .

Just Write _____

_____

_____

_____

_____

_____

_____

_____

_____

_____

_____

You Have The POWER To Create New, Positive
Habits And Let Go Of The Old, Outdated Ways.

When you Have More to Say . . .

Just Write _____

_____

_____

_____

_____

_____

_____

_____

_____

_____

_____

_____

We are not on this path to fix ourselves,
but to become the best version of ourselves
that we can be. There is a difference.

The Ruts In The Road That Keep You Stuck

Journalling Exercise

What habitual patterns are you noticing that you're repeating in your life experiences today? *This includes thoughts, words, and actions which contribute to your belief systems. Write them down.*

_____

_____

_____

_____

_____

What patterns are you experiencing today, that you might remember seeing in your parents, caregivers, or grandparents?

_____

_____

_____

_____

_____

The Ruts In The Road That Keep You Stuck

Make sure to apply the *"no judgement rule"* and look at yourself, your parents/caregivers, and grandparents with love and compassion. Just like you, they may not have been aware of their limiting beliefs and patterns, either.

The origins of these patterns often began from hardships and traumatic life experiences by your ancestors. These patterns can be inherited and handed down through generations. This means you came into this world, "pre-programmed." Baggage that was never really yours from the start!

The subconscious mind records every life experience you have. That's everything you do, say, feel, and think. The next time something happens that your subconscious deems "unsafe," it will do everything in its power to keep you safe, especially if what you're doing is taking you entirely out of your comfort zone.

The unknown can be scary! Being unaware of this at a conscious level, you can end up in self-sabotaging behaviour, feeling stuck and unable to move out of this pattern.

By practicing **awareness,** you have the POWER to create new positive habits and let go of the old ones to get unstuck and move forward feeling, EMPOWERED!

When you Have More to Say . . .

Just Write _____

_____

_____

_____

_____

_____

_____

_____

_____

_____

_____

_____

_____

Is That Baggage Really Yours?

When you Have More to Say . . .

Just Write _____

_____

_____

_____

_____

_____

_____

_____

_____

_____

_____

_____

_____

Clear Your Inner Clutter

WE COMPLICATE LIFE WHEN WE LOOK PAST THE SIMPLICITY OF THINGS

Play Sheet

Let Love Be Your Guide

Let Love be Your Guide

What if you saw everything through the lens of love?

When we implement the tools and strategies available for us to use, like breaking through a wall, we can break through what we perceive to be our limits and realize there are no limits.

We are infinite, and we only limit ourselves by getting bogged down by the mental and emotional clutter, our blocks, and limiting belief systems.

When we choose to see everything through the lens of love versus fear-based thoughts, words, actions, and reactions, our world opens to a whole new reality that becomes more joyous, abundant, and full of possibilities.

After all, if you're always thinking anyway, why not think positive (love-based) thoughts and create your life on purpose with more joy, rather than creating your experiences by attracting a fear-based reality and self-fulfilling prophecies?

Remember, you *always* have the POWER to make a different choice.

AWARENESS IS KEY TO GETTING UNSTUCK AND MOVING FORWARD, ONE STEP AT A TIME.

What If You Saw Everything Through The
Lens Of Love? - The Practice -

Before working through these questions, use the power tool, "1, 2, 3, Breathe," included in the Power Tools Section.

When you're feeling the spiral of mental and emotional clutter, ask yourself these questions:

- Have I used the power tool 1, 2, 3, Breathe before continuing with the questions?

- What emotions am I feeling right now?

- Why am I feeling these emotions right now?

- Am I thinking of something in the future that hasn't happened yet?

- Am I thinking of something that happened in the past and I cannot change?

- Is this something happening in the present moment?

- Have I acknowledged and honoured myself for how I'm feeling?

- Am I ready to let these feelings go? If not, why not?

- How can I perceive this situation differently in order to let these feelings go?

- Am I looking at this situation through the lens of love or is it fear-based?

What If You Saw Everything Through The Lens Of Love?
- The Practice –

Whatever the situation is, developing the habit of taking yourself through the list of questions can result in a better outcome.

Slow and mindful breathing is calming and interrupts what's known as the *"fight or flight"* system from going off like a fire alarm when you are feeling any anxiety, stress, or panic. Your internal alarm system instantly sets off a chemical chain reaction within your body, raising your cortisol and insulin levels. Over time, this can lead to adrenal burnout, sleepless nights, and even overeating and weight gain.

Hold a loving and compassionate space for yourself as you go through any healing process. Do not stuff your emotions down to bury them. Allow yourself to feel your emotions without judgement knowing that it is a necessary part of the healing process and your growth.

What If You Saw Everything Through
The Lens Of Love?
– The Practice –

Take Action

Use the list of questions on the previous page as a guide to help you work through any situations. Use the following journalling pages to record your thoughts and feelings.

Often, situations can be resolved by journalling and expressing your emotions. Each time you take yourself through this checklist and journal the insights received, you:

✓ Create an opportunity to anchor and focus on the present moment.

✓ Create an opportunity to journal and receive insights into the present situation.

✓ Create an opportunity to release any stuck emotions in your body.

✓ Create an opportunity to feel free and clear to take action.

So much flows to you
through GRATITUDE

When you Have More to Say . . .

Just Write _____

_____

_____

_____

_____

_____

_____

_____

_____

_____

_____

_____

When I Let Go, I Attract Miracles

When you Have More to Say . . .

Just Write _____

_____

_____

_____

_____

_____

_____

_____

_____

_____

_____

_____

_____

Be Authentically, Soulfully You

When you Have More to Say . . .

Just Write _____

_____

_____

_____

_____

_____

_____

_____

_____

_____

_____

Life Is Beautiful

Remember to fall in love with yourself

Play Sheet

Ho'oponopono

Healing Through Forgiveness

Ho'oponopono - Introduction

"Healing through "Forgiveness"

Known as the ancient practice of forgiveness and
reconciliation, Ho'oponopono is the simple practice
for healing current or past relationships with anyone,
including the relationship you have with yourself.

This powerful Ho'oponopono clearing technique
can be used to heal issues, addictions, or
any challenges you're currently facing.

It doesn't need to be complicated; it's the power
of the energy and intention behind it.
It's beautiful and it works!

I'm sorry
Please forgive me
Thank you
I love you

Ho'oponopono - Introduction

"Healing through "Forgiveness"

What is it you want to heal and release? Food addictions? Alcoholism? Smoking? The heartache from a broken relationship or the loss of a loved one? Anger issues? Health problems? What emotions have you been stuffing down inside your body to avoid facing? This could be something consciously or subconsciously, that is holding you back from moving on with life.

Whether it is known or unknown to you, Ho'oponopono works – peeling away the layers of unreconciled pain, fear, and anything else you haven't healed. That's why this beautiful practice works so well.

Ho'oponopono - The Practice

"Healing through "Forgiveness"

The Ho'oponopono practice is beautiful for changing and clearing the energy surrounding something or someone specific, and then bring on healing. It doesn't matter what it is or how long ago it happened. If you want to know if there is something that needs healing, then try the practice.

Four simple phrases with a lot of impact! *The meaning behind the simple, yet powerful phrases:*

I'm sorry: Remorse, sadness, regret for something that took place; known or unknown to you.

Please forgive me: Offering forgiveness to the other person, yourself, or the energy of the situation. This is the act of *unburdening* yourself from the toxic energy created by your emotions tied to the situation.

Thank you: Gratitude for yourself, others, whatever your focus is; it can be known or unknown. Perhaps it's giving thanks to the Universe, or thanking your body for supporting you, it doesn't matter, just say "thank you."

I love you: Love is a powerful thing and it's everything! There is a lot of power and energy behind saying the phrase "I love you." Whatever your focus has been through this process, make sure to say, "I love you."

Ho'oponopono - The Practice

"Healing through "Forgiveness"

Take the time to go through this process when you can be alone and focus your intentions on it.

It can get ugly; rant, scream, cry, swear, whatever it takes to heal and release the stuck emotions and clear the energy once and for all. It's probably long overdue.

It's also important to understand that whatever happened in the past and whatever actions took place, by using Ho'oponopono you are not condoning the act by any person for any reason. Using Ho'oponopono allows for the toxic energy to be released from within your energy, and your body, so you can move on with living your best life.

Take Action

Ho'oponopono is a powerful clearing technique. Use it until you feel the heaviness of your emotions shift and you feel lighter. Then, journal using the pages that follow to capture any thoughts you receive from the experience. It can be insightful and is a valuable part of the healing process.

Tip! Have a box of tissue handy. You may use it a lot.

Ho'oponopono – The Practice

"Healing through Forgiveness"

- Focus on whatever it is you want to take through this process. Refer to the previous examples, but it is not limited to these; it can be any person, place, or thing. It can be a present moment situation in your daily life that you, yourself is dealing with.

- Repeat the four phrases. The energy will become heavy as the emotions well up within you. Keep saying the phrases until you feel the energy lighten and you feel free and clear to move on.

- You can mix up the phrases and still feel the shift and see the results. Remember, it's the energy, focus, and intention you put behind this practice.

- When you feel the emotions well up inside you, don't stuff them back down but let them come up to be released. This is a vital part of the healing process.

> This is a powerful process to use on yourself where YOU are the focus of forgiveness to bring on healing so you can move forward unhindered. Free.

I'm sorry ♥ Please forgive me ♥ Thank you ♥ I love you

When you Have More to Say . . .

Just Write _____

_____

_____

_____

_____

_____

_____

_____

_____

_____

_____

_____

_____

_____

_____

Life is Beautiful

When you Have More to Say . . .

Just Write _____

_____

_____

_____

_____

_____

_____

_____

_____

_____

_____

_____

Love Yourself More

When you Have More to Say . . .

Just Write _____

_____

_____

_____

_____

_____

_____

_____

_____

_____

_____

_____

_____

_____

I'm sorry ♥ Please forgive me ♥ Thank you ♥ I love you

Only look back to see how far you've come.

30 Day
Self-Reflection Summary

When the world says
"Give up,"
Hope whispers,
"try it one more time."

Reflecting on the Last 30 Days

30 Days of Reflection - Summary Instructions

Summarize

Look through the weekly gratitude sections, including the weekly reflections journalling that you've done over the past 30 days. On the following pages, use the prompts to summarize the most significant changes, shifts, and insights that took place for you since you began this journey.

Celebrate and acknowledge how far you've come!

By doing the exercises, you will:

✓ Anchor in the positive experiences you've had.

✓ Continue rewiring your brain for more positive shifts in your thinking and uplift your vibe.

✓ Receive new insights and *aha* moments as you read through the last 30 days. Journal them!

✓ Continue to grow your awareness and reinforce that your daily practices are working!

✓ Realize how much you've transformed both your internal and external world.

✓ Feel more gratitude for yourself, your experiences, and the little things you've captured, including the blessings from any challenging situations you may have encountered.

"Gratitude opens the door to the power,
the wisdom, the creativity of the Universe.
you open the door through gratitude."

Deepak Chopra

Reflecting on the Last 30 Days

WHAT are you especially grateful for this month?

_____

_____

_____

_____

Why?

_____

_____

_____

WHO are you especially grateful for this month?

_____

_____

_____

_____

Why?

_____

_____

_____

Reflecting on the Last 30 Days

If there was a time you struggled with feeling grateful over the last 30 days, why? *What happened that you felt this way?*

_____

_____

_____

_____

_____

How did you overcome it?

_____

_____

_____

_____

_____

Learning to focus on gratitude when you least feel like it, is when you need to use it most.

Remember to use journalling to express your feelings and release them from your body. Use the following journalling page to continue writing.

Continue to use the Power Tools and Play Sheets. It will help you move through any difficulties.

Reflecting on the Last 30 Days

Journalling supports you in receiving clarity and further insights, continue writing!

_____

_____

_____

_____

_____

_____

_____

_____

_____

_____

Refer to the play sheet, "Ho'oponopono," the ancient practice of forgiveness. It will help you to release any lingering, uncomfortable feelings.

"Wear gratitude like a cloak and it will feed every area of your life"
-Rumi

Reflecting on the Last 30 Days

What changes have you noticed in yourself over the past 30 days?

_____

_____

_____

_____

_____

How has opening up to feeling more gratitude this month made a difference for you?

_____

_____

_____

_____

_____

"GRATITUDE IS THE SINGLE MOST IMPORTANT INGREDIENT
TO LIVING A SUCCESSFUL AND FULFILLED LIFE."
Jack Canfield

Reflecting on the Last 30 Days

What shifts in perspective and your mindset have you noticed over the past 30 days?

_____

_____

_____

_____

_____

_____

_____

_____

_____

_____

_____

_____

_____

What You FOCUS On Gets More Powerful.

When you Have More to Say . . .

Just Write _____

_____

_____

_____

_____

_____

_____

_____

_____

_____

_____

_____

Let Go, And Let The Universe Do Its Thing!

Reflecting on the Last 30 days

Capturing Synchronicities

From your weekly reflection pages, what were the BIGGEST synchronicities or opportunities that presented themselves to you that you were aware of and took action on? *Summarize them:*

_____

_____

_____

_____

_____

_____

_____

_____

_____

_____

_____

Journalling Offers Clarity And Insights

When you Have More to Say . . .

Just Write _____

_____

_____

_____

_____

_____

_____

_____

_____

_____

_____

_____

_____

_____

I DON'T HAVE TO CHASE
EXTRAORDINARY
MOMENTS TO FIND
HAPPINESS -
IT'S RIGHT IN FRONT OF
ME IF I'M PAYING
ATTENTION AND
PRACTICING GRATITUDE.

Reflecting on the Last 30 days

Capturing The Positive Changes

What experiences stand out the most for you, where you used the tools and strategies to help you overcome a challenge and then move on? *Briefly describe those experiences here.*

_____

_____

_____

_____

_____

_____

_____

_____

_____

_____

Be Open To Something New

When you Have More to Say . . .

Just Write _____

_____

_____

_____

_____

_____

_____

_____

_____

_____

_____

_____

_____

_____

_____

I Listen, I Trust, I Take Guided Action

Reflecting on the Last 30 days

Capturing The Positive Changes

Overall, how has this 30-day journey impacted you and your life? *What's different now?*

_____

_____

_____

_____

_____

_____

_____

_____

_____

_____

_____

_____

Ask Yourself Questions To Receive Answers

When you Have More to Say . . .

Just Write _____

_____

_____

_____

_____

_____

_____

_____

_____

_____

_____

_____

_____

I Listen, I Trust, I Take Guided Action

gratitude
helps you
fall in love
with the life

you already have

and

from that place

you attract so much

more

Your Personal Declaration

Affirm your commitment to continue moving forward on this beautiful, soulful journey of yours. There is more growth, more rewards, more joy for you to experience!

When you sign this promise to yourself, you're sending a message to the Universe that you're ready to receive more healing, growth, abundance, and success!

> I commit to:
> Continuing my gratitude practices
> and my soul journey.

I commit to honouring myself and where I am in my journey without judgement or comparing myself to others.

I commit to taking small actionable steps and celebrate what I accomplish – not focus on what I haven't.

I commit to opening my heart to feeling more joy and self-love.

I commit to showing up for myself and doing the inner work for my well-being and growth.

I welcome abundance into my life.

I welcome miracles into my life.

Signed _____ Date _____

Let's Celebrate!

Congratulations!

You Took Action and Completed…

**The Energy of Gratitude and More,
30-Day Take Action Journal!**

Honour and Celebrate your Accomplishment!

Keep the Momentum Going!

Set an intention to continue with the
daily gratitude practices and journalling.

Repeat this take action journal for
new experiences and continued growth.

About Lauryn

Lauryn's training is the culmination of years of study in a wide variety of disciplines, including, metaphysical, spiritual, mindset, and two health coaching certifications.

With inner transformation as the goal, she inspires others to do the inner work and uncover the root causes of their clutter. The common thread often appears as a combination of mental and emotional clutter (fear, doubt, worry, procrastination), mindset, and limiting beliefs.

"This inner chaos and confusion are reflected in one's outer world clogging up their lives, keeping them from achieving their dreams and reaching their full potential."

Lauryn Senko

Through her coaching and product creation, Lauryn combines her love for learning with her passion for writing and creating courses, journals, planners, inspirational card decks, digital products, and more. Always focusing on helping others to take action one small step at a time toward living their life on purpose, in alignment, and with more joy.

"Writing this book has been an inner soul journey for me. Reading it and taking action on what you learn in this guide can propel you to greater heights on yours!"

Thank You!

I am deeply honoured you chose my book to accompany you on your journey of growth and self-discovery. Thank you for putting your trust and faith in me, yourself and the Universe!

Got a Moment?
I'd be grateful for feedback on Amazon!

Please share a brief review on Amazon. What did you enjoy most about this journal? Your input will help me and future readers.

TESTIMONIAL
If you found this Take Action Journal helpful, I would be grateful if you would take *5 minutes* to provide me with a short testimonial of your experience:

ClutterClearingDiva.com/EOGTestimonial

BECOME A VIP INSIDER!
Receive: Discounts, Freebies & Enriching Content. Stay on top of new product releases.

Sign up at:
ClutterClearingDiva.com/VIPINSIDER

CONNECT WITH ME
Instagram.com/ClutterClearingDiva
Facebook.com/ClutterClearingDiva
ClutterClearingDiva.com

Next Steps

IMAGINE
your dreams

CREATE

your happiness

LIVE
your life

Enrich The Journey!

The Energy of Gratitude and More, 21-Day Take Action Gratitude Challenge

JOIN THE CHALLENGE - SIGN UP NOW!

When You Participate in the 21-Day Take Action, Gratitude Challenge You Will:

- ✓ Learn how gratitude is a SUPERPOWER, amplifying your vibration & manifesting powers!
- ✓ Learn how to become expansive in your energy, opening you up to the flow of the Universe.
- ✓ Learn how to naturally cultivate a positive attitude dissolving your "inner clutter" (mental & emotional clutter of doubt, fears, worries, negativity & more.)
- ✓ Be inspired to deepen your daily gratitude practice by using the Power Tools & Play Sheets in my book, The Energy of Gratitude and More, 30 Day Take Action Journal.
- ✓ Learn new concepts not taught in the book and most of all, have FUN & RAISE YOUR VIBE!

This challenge is for everyone whether or not you have read, "The Energy of Gratitude and More," so consider participating and enrich your journey!

CHECK IT OUT HERE:
ClutterClearingDiva.com/GratitudeChallenge21

Continue the Journey

CURRENT PUBLICATIONS

**The Energy of Gratitude and More,
30 Day Take Action Journal**
*Mindfully Manifest Your Desires & Co-Create
Your Life with the Universe, Uncluttered & On Purpose.*

<u>Lined Journals with Quotes</u>
**When You Have More To Say, Just Write!
You Were Meant to Shine
Believe In Yourself**

COMING IN 2021

**The Energy of Gratitude and More,
30 Day Take Action Journal**
Digital & Kindle version

<u>E-Courses & Challenges</u>

**21 Day Gratitude Challenge
The "Vibe" (Vision) Board Challenge
The Energy of Gratitude E-Course
Change Your Mindset, Transform Your Life
E-Course**

<u>Inspirational Card Decks</u>

"The Energy of Gratitude and More" Card Deck
Receive daily, uplifting inspiration by pulling a card a day!

What you **THINK**, you become

What you **FEEL**, you attract

What you **IMAGINE**, you create

– Buddha

What will you create today?

Follow Me

Clear Your "Inner Clutter"

Instagram.com/ClutterClearingDiva

It all starts with one small step, keep going!

Printed in the United States
by Baker & Taylor Publisher Services